KEEP FOLK SMILING AGAIN

The Houghton Weavers' Story

TONY BERRY

peakpublish

Peak Publish
An imprint of Peak Platform New Bridge, Calver, Hope Valley,
Derbyshire S32 3XT

First published by Peak Publish 2015
Text Copyright Tony Berry
All rights reserved
The moral right of the authors has been asserted
Cover Design Balaji M
Printed in England

A CIP catalogue record for this book is available from the British
Library

ISBN: 978-1-907219-37-5
www.peakplatform.com

With acknowledgements to all who
contributed to this tale

To Elizabeth

With love,

Tony Benn x

Dedicated to Andrea

Keep Folk Smiling Again

"I'd like to come tonight, if that's possible?"

"Possible, it's absolutely marvellous!"

That was Terry Wheeler calling me! He was a BBC television producer and he had arranged to see us the previous night. Unfortunately the night was a total wash out. We were bad, the sound was bad, the audience were awful and we came away thinking the guy had been and gone! Fortunately he couldn't make it, so there we were arranging another possible meeting.

"No problem Terry! We are singing at Sharples High School in Bolton, so when you get there, there will be tickets at the door in your name."

"Thanks! I'll see you there tonight!"

Brilliant! We'd been given another chance. We thought we'd better not let it slip away from us this time.

I'd better explain. My name is Tony Berry and I'm the singer in a folk group. I live in Westhoughton, a town almost equidistant between Bolton and Wigan in the fair county of Lancashire; well it was in Lancashire until 1974, when some faceless people in Whitehall decided to change the boundaries and put us into 'Greater Manchester'. They also decided that we should become part of Bolton as well. To a certain degree I don't mind that 'cos I'm a big Wanderers fan but we don't really need a 'big brother' as we are big enough to look after ourselves! As far as the 'Friends of Real Lancashire' are concerned, we're still 'Lanky', so that'll do for me!

We take our name from the town of my birth; a place that had several weaving sheds when I was growing up; hence the Westhoughton Weavers. That lasted about two gigs when we

1

chopped off the 'west', as it was a bit of a mouthful and became, "The Houghton Weavers". Maybe that name was chosen because the most famous folk group at the time were the 'Spinners' from Liverpool, Spinners/Weavers? That particular group almost certainly chose their name following mega folk group from America called the 'Weavers' led by legendary singer, Pete Seeger. I've never liked the name but it stuck and I'm quite happy to live with it.

The group I played with had been going for a couple of years at that point and had built up a reasonable reputation in our locality. The group consisted of myself, Norman, who told the gags and David and Denis, brothers who played guitar and bass respectively. David and Denis' mum, Gladys, wrote to the BBC to ask if they would have a look at this up and coming group in the hope that they could be considered for a programme called "We'll Call You!" This is a show that allowed the viewing public to see acts from around the region that had no previous television exposure. The show's producer, Terry Wheeler, was to have a look at us to see if we would be possible material for the show.

We'd not a lot of time to get ourselves psyched up as he was coming that night! Maybe that was a good thing? It didn't leave us much time to worry ourselves to death. We could only be ourselves and try to entertain as best we could – no use trying to be something we weren't! A quick phone call to tell everybody what was happening, then it was time to get your thinking caps on to decide what material to use in the show. We'd by this time gathered together a multitude of songs, so it was decision time as to what would go down best with our audience that night. We had learned over the previous couple of years that a show uses a certain formula, that's difficult to create but once found you can use it time and again. In other words, you start with a certain type of song, followed by a certain type of song, etc; the ballad will probably go in third or fourth place, the comedy song will follow that and so on. The hard bit is to choose which songs fit the bill in each particular instance. You pick a list of material, change it several times, agree on a final draft, change that a couple of times; then just before you go on stage you alter it again! Once you come off stage and things haven't gone as planned you'll argue with

2

each other as to whether the amendments were justified or sensible! If the evening is a success, it's due to your diligence in choosing the right material!

We'd already built up quite a repertoire of material through necessity. Running several weekly folk clubs in the area had meant that it was imperative to constantly learn new songs. You couldn't turn up every week and sing the same songs or people would soon get bored. We'd listen to albums of our favourite artists and learn a couple of songs from each. One or two songs were written by members of the group and people who wrote songs began sending them to us in the hope we might play them. Finally, in our weekly clubs we'd hire guests for the evening who'd be singing songs that we might not have heard. If we enjoyed a particular one, we'd ask if they minded if we added it to our collection. I've always found it strange in folk music, that some artists don't like other people singing their songs. In every other genre of music, writers would be extremely pleased that other people would be singing their songs but not always for the "folkies". Some want to be the only people in the world that sing that particular song.....strange!

Our evening in Bolton was going to be a sell out so that was a great start. We were already building a reasonable following, the odd newspaper article, word of mouth and sales of our recent album. Although we've never sung at this school before, we were all confident that things would go well – it couldn't be worse than the previous night! We planned to arrive earlier than usual so that everything was checked – we mustn't have a problem with the sound like the night before. In fact, we didn't want anything to be like the previous night so we needed to get that out of our minds! Give 'em a good night's entertainment and they can only like what they see and hear.......................we hoped!

Sharples High School

So we arrived early and set up our gear. We had two old speakers and a heavy, old fashioned amplifier and mixing desk. Denis was the electrician in the group so it was up to him to make us sound okay. All the gear was packed into the boot of the cars. I couldn't drive at the time, so that was the responsibility of the other three. I concentrated on the songs whilst Norman's forte was the joke telling! We'd more or less decided on our repertoire for the evening, including the gags. Our reputation in the area was building and we were expecting an attentive audience. It was utter bliss for me when an audience sat and listened to our act. I'd done a few years of solo work in the Social Clubs around the area and that was tough! In some places they would talk all night, even if Frank Sinatra was top of the bill! Folk clubs were a different kettle of fish. They expected the audience to be quiet whilst the entertainers were performing and would tell off anyone who overstepped the mark – a lot of teachers were 'folkies' so they must have felt they were still in the classroom!

Right, first things first! Where to put the speakers to get the best sound? Should we re-arrange the seating so that everyone was facing us? That sounds rather an obvious thing to expect but don't believe it. I'm sure some organisers turn the chairs around so that folk can have a chat whilst we are playing! Had we chosen the right things to wear and the best songs to sing? Then, I thought, oh, for God's sake, Tony, stop worrying and enjoy the night. If he didn't like it, he didn't like it! There's nothing we could do about that. Just do your best, as my mother used to say. She had been sitting at home, rosary beads

4

in hand, praying that the Good Lord would make my voice sound like an angel!

As we had been brought up in a strong Roman Catholic family, we attended mass every Sunday, Benediction on a Wednesday and were expected to attend every church fund-raising occasion! I'd been an altar boy and when I passed the eleven plus and went to grammar school, I realised what a backwater I'd come from. We started school aged five and most left aged fifteen with no qualifications whatsoever. That wasn't because they'd failed their exams; there were no exams to fail! They didn't take any; and so left school without any form of educational start in life. I, on the other hand attended a school that expected GCE passes and A levels giving me a better chance than my mates left behind in Westhoughton.

Sharples School was an example of how education had progressed during the previous twenty years. A new secondary school with all the facilities needed for a kid to progress. It must be a pleasure to go there every day....then again, let's not get carried away, it's still school!

"We'll put one speaker on the top of that old piano and the other one can go on the vaulting horse near the entrance to the gym." Yes, gym; we were singing in the sports hall! All the tables and chairs were arranged like a cabaret night, with candles on each table to create an atmosphere! There would be potato pie and peas in the interval, which would be served from the dining room next door. The sound would bounce around this room so we would need to speak clearly so that he, what's his name again, can understand us. The organisers were getting just as nervous as we were. They knew the potential of the evening, so there was encouragement flying round the room in bucket loads!

"Don't worry lads, we'll cheer every song and laugh at every joke!"

"Thanks! But please don't overdo things!"

Slowly the helpers trickled in followed, eventually, by the audience. There was a bustle of excitement as they all received the news that a BBC executive was coming to watch the show. I'd made up my mind what he would look like; green corduroy trousers with brown brogues on his feet, striped cheesecloth shirt with a mass of long curly brown hair, probably a duffle coat and glasses. He'll be around the six foot mark and talk with an 'ever so far back' accent and be utterly condescending. I wasn't bothered about any of that as long as he enjoyed the show.

When he eventually arrived I found that I was right in only one aspect and that was the accent; BBC through and through! Medium height, dressed in a suit, balding, white hair, well a bit of white hair! extremely likeable, though nervous with a 'don't suffer fools lightly' attitude. This was to be the bloke who would become our friend and mentor over the next few years, although, at the time, he looked altogether terrifying! He carried a briefcase which he opened to reveal a clip board with paper and pen attached. It was beginning to feel like my 'O' & 'A' levels all rolled into one!

Attached to the clip board was the letter sent to the BBC by David and Denis's mother, Gladys.

Terry re-read the letter and commented, "Well she thinks very highly of you!"

"Well she is my mother", replied Denis. "I hope she's right!" added Terry. So did I! I hoped it was the most truthful thing that Gladys had ever said. After several minutes of talking 'showbiz' that went completely over my head, Terry decided to take his place in the audience. Fortunately for us, the organisers asked if we were ready to start, which gave us no time to panic. We were introduced and went on stage. From that point onwards memories of the night remain a total blank in my mind. We must have gone down well because he stayed the whole night and came backstage at the end to congratulate us on our performance. On leaving, Terry thanked us and said he would be back in touch in the very near future.

So that was it! Waiting for months and it was all over in a flash. We'll probably never see him again, we thought – maybe a call from his secretary to say that we weren't what they were looking for. Not to worry, I thought, I can tell my kids, if I ever have any, that we once had a television producer watching us and he quite liked what he saw!

So we begin to pack away all the gear before leaving for home.

"Well, what do you think?" asked David.

"He seemed to like it but you never know. Let's not get carried away", retorted Norman.

"I know what we should do!" I replied. "What's that?" "Let's go to the pub!"

Back to Normal

So, it was back to work the following day but I just couldn't stop thinking about the previous night. I'm sure you've been in the same situation, where an occurrence of some sort just won't leave your brain and life seems to be totally revolving around something that has no relevance to what you're doing at the time.

But I had to try and forget it for the time being and concentrate on other things like work, football and Westhoughton! That's the town of my birth and I love it! It has a rich history, dating back many hundreds of years. But I can't stop thinking about the lure of fame and fortune! One such person probably felt the same way some two centuries before. He was probably more concerned with the fortune rather than the fame, or in this case, infamy! His name was Richard Lockett and he built the most modern mill in the world.

200 years ago, Europe was in turmoil. Britain had recently ended its wars with Russia and Sweden to join forces with them, to fight the Little General, Napoleon Bonaparte. He, in turn, had decided to invade Russia during the winter. Wellington was fighting in Spain during the Peninsular War and Admiral Lord Nelson had recently fought and died at Trafalgar. Attempts to stop trade with France led to the 1812 war with the United States. England was to suffer the only assassination of a Prime Minister and Charles Dickens, who would tell tales of workhouses, famine and deprivation, was born.

With this as a background, a major revolution was taking place in agriculture, transportation, mining and manufacturing. This was to take many decades but would change the way

Britain and the world would behave thereafter. Steam and water power, railways and canals, all added to the speed of this revolution. In textiles, several inventions by Arkwright (water frame), Hargreaves (spinning jenny) and Samuel Crompton (spinning mule) revolutionised the industry and led to an enormous increase in the output of yarn.

In Lancashire, the quiet life of the handloom weaver was about to be blown apart. These weavers had their own, or rented looms, within their households and the whole family were involved in the production of cloth. For many years these new developments didn't threaten them, as cloth was still in high demand and they could earn very good wages.

The first power loom was built in 1785 and developed over the next 50 years until, eventually, it was totally automatic. There was a lot of money to be made and mills began to spring up everywhere. As the cloth became more abundant the price began a downwards spiral forcing the handloom weaver out of business.

In the sleepy suburbs of Lancashire the handloom weavers were happily plying their trade whilst big business lay in the wings about to make as much money as they could. Money would be pumped into the local economy and the rich would get richer, at the expense of these local tradesmen.

Westhoughton was a sleeping giant, destined to become a boom town during this first decade of the 19th Century as mill owners decided that here is where the newest machinery in the world would be used. There would be work for the people of the town and the handloom weavers could either take it or leave it!

These men, working in small family groups, began to band together and form associations to protect their livelihoods. In retaliation the government banned unions and gave the power back to the already powerful bosses. Food prices rocketed, widespread unemployment was rife and the working classes blamed the introduction of power looms for their misery. Anger was rising amongst these workers who were now so destitute that they would go days without food. Taxes were high, to support the wars we were involved in, people pawned everything they had to prop up their miserable existence. Armed militia began to roam the streets led by cavalry, who

9

used swords rather than words to control a crowd. Don't forget, it was to be over 50 years before Custer's last Stand at the Little Big Horn or when Jesse James and Billy the Kid terrorised the Wild West. Times were hard. You survived or were sent to the workhouse to face hardship, embarrassment, destitution and almost certain death. What do you do – you fight for your rights and freedom.

In Nottinghamshire, similar problems were surfacing and the unemployed workforce got together secretly to form an amalgamation of protestors that became known as the Luddites. This name came from a mythical character who, like Robin Hood, lived in Sherwood Forest. He was known as King Ludd or General Ludd. The movement spread throughout the new industrial areas in England including Lancashire and secret meetings took place, late at night, in the moorlands surrounding the industrial areas. The Luddites had begun to destroy the new power looms in the mills and an act of Parliament in February (the Frame breaking Act of 1812) made it an offence to damage power looms and was punishable by death.

The Burning of Westhoughton Mill

In 1804, a mill was built in Westhoughton by Richard Lockett, who lived at Westhoughton Hall. It was filled with the newest machinery that money could buy including 170 pairs of power looms. The mill was leased to Messrs Rowe and Duncough in 1806. It employed a large number of local people but the skills needed to work the machinery were far less than the experienced hand-loom weavers. By 1812 it was becoming increasingly obvious that the mill would become a target for these disillusioned Luddites. The Royal Scots Grey cavalry were deployed to defend the mill from these dissenters. They were based in Bolton some five miles away.

Things were getting worse for the general populace. It was reported that the poorest were resorting to eating nettles as a replacement for potatoes which were too expensive. Food riots had taken place in Bolton, Mr. George Perceval, the Prime minister, was assassinated in London and the secret Luddite meetings came to the conclusion that Westhoughton Mill should be burned to the ground. On Friday morning, on the 24th April, there were rumours of a planned attack on the mill. The Scots Greys were sent for but when they arrived, all was quiet. Their leader, Captain Bullen, assumed it was a hoax and returned to Bolton.

By midday, a crowd had begun to gather and the mob proceeded to the factory. They broke into the unguarded mill, smashed the machinery, wrapped the cloth around the wooden looms and using a hogshead of tallow as a fire-lighter, burned the place to the ground. A young lad called Abraham

Charleson went to the stables of the White Lion pub to fetch a handful of straw to assist the conflagration. Westhoughton Hall, the home of the mill owner, was also burned to the ground on the same day. Once the fire had fully established itself the rabble decided to make a run for it The Scots Greys were about to return and the magistrates were reading the riot act in order to disperse the mob.

The military very quickly rounded up anyone they felt might have been responsible and all were arrested. Eventually twenty four men and two women were tried at Lancaster. The trial found four of them guilty of the greater charge of setting fire to the mill and they were sentenced to hang. Job Fletcher (aged 34), Thomas Kerfoot (26), James Smith (31) and the boy, Abraham Charleson who was reputed to be 16 but whose parents insisted was only 12 were hanged outside Lancaster Castle on the 13th June. It is reported that Abraham cried for his mother before his execution.

Nine of the prisoners were convicted of taking or administering an illegal oath and were transported to Australia for seven years, although one died on the journey and another was considered too old to be of use in the penal colony so served his sentence in Hampshire.

The Luddite movement, although trying to help the skilled workforce actually caused a considerable amount of hardship to the town of Westhoughton. No entrepreneur would invest in the town for many decades making life in the town intolerable for the average working man.

The Lights of Broadway?

I, on the other hand, two centuries later, found my home town of Westhoughton a marvellous place. Everything seemed to be working out well and life was good. I was living at home with my mother at the time. Lots of people called me 'mummy's boy' as I didn't leave home until I was thirty two years old. I had no problem with the name calling; my mother made all my meals, washed and ironed all my clothes and made my life easy. That was until the day I was dashing around to get ready to go out. I called to my mother from the bathroom, "Mum, can you see that shirt hanging in the kitchen. Will you iron it please 'cos I'm in a bit of a hurry?"

After bathing, I walked into the living room to see my shirt hanging from the same coat hanger in the kitchen. "Thanks a lot!" I shout, "I told you I was in a hurry!" I then proceeded to get out the ironing board and the iron and pressed my shirt before bidding a hasty farewell.

A couple of days later I asked 'mater' if she'd oblige me by ironing a shirt.

"Not on your life!" came her reply, "Two days ago you asked me to iron a shirt and I did. When you came down, you obviously thought I'd not done a good enough job and ironed it again!!"

"So you'd already ironed that shirt for me?"

"Yes, of course, but don't worry, I'll not be ironing anything else for you!"

And that was the last word on the matter. She never did iron another shirt for me again!

I didn't hold it against her at all. I became quite proficient at ironing and you will still find me pressing all my own clothes, however I never got round to making my own dresses! Working, playing and singing still continued at a pace but the lure of the television screen was never far from my thoughts.

London Palladium here we come! Top of the Pops! The world was our oyster!

But I'm not too keen on oysters! It's not real food.....you don't chew it....just swallow it and it's gone! Maybe like the dreams I'm having.....look and you've missed it. It leaves you in a kind of limbo, where you don't want to start something off in case someone knocks at the door. A bit like the bloke who's coming to mend your cooker. You sit at home all day in the hope that he'll arrive. You daren't start anything or he'll turn up. So you wait in all day and at five o'clock he rings to say he'll be there first thing tomorrow!

So I went through the motions, waiting for that phone call...........and after a few days it happened!

"Hello there, it's Terry from the BBC. We've sorted out the schedule and you'll be recording the third show of the series. Can you be there from lunch time?"

Lunch time! I'll stay all night just to get a chance!

"You'll be performing two songs with a bit of chat in between. My secretary will ring with more details but I'll look forward to seeing you then."

People call me a dreamer but sometimes dreams can come true!

So for the next couple of weeks we were obsessed by the thought of our television future. Would it be worthwhile, would it be successful, would we make fools of ourselves? It reminds me of one bloke who said that television is a device that lets people with nothing to do watch people who can't do anything! I hope it's not like that.

We tried our damndest to be normal but the all consuming thought that a big break may be near filled all our thoughts. Work, for me at the time, was an Adult Training Centre for adults with learning difficulties. I was called an instructor and helped with the daily routine of the establishment. The centre had several contracts with the National Health Service. The students assembled an emergency first aid kit containing a bandage, several balls of wool, a sling and other necessities contained in a foil tray. When assembled they would be taken away to be sterilised. Other rooms had educational classes or needlework and sewing. Some of the students made woollen toys which would be sold to raise much needed revenue. These students were classed as 'handicapped' but it always made me chuckle. Every morning they would arrive with smiles on their faces and at three in the afternoon would depart with those same grins covering their visage. I, on the other hand, would walk around with the cares of the world on my shoulders, thinking of everything that might make life worse. I felt better when I reflected who was the handicapped person, them or me? Isn't everyone handicapped in some way or another? It is just the general attitude of people that gives these labels. Even people with good health and lots of money might feel handicapped in comparison to someone else. Many major celebrities over recent years have 'come out' about mental health issues that have affected their lives. People can't see this handicap and so in many ways it is overlooked. Some go into deep holes of depression that most people could not understand with quips like 'they've got everything so why are they complaining'. It's not that they are complaining but trying to get people to understand the darker side of life.

One of the funniest men around was 'Goon', Spike Milligan, who suffered severe bipolar disorder throughout his life and had at least ten mental breakdowns. He spoke very candidly about his condition, saying that at times he could not stand to be awake as the pain was too much. When television honoured Spike in 1994, he interrupted the Prince of Wales, who was giving a glowing report of the man, by calling him a 'grovelling little bastard!' Prince Charles was a great friend of his and Spike faxed him after the programme asking "I suppose a knighthood is out of the question?" He was made an honorary Knight Commander of the Order of the British Empire (KBE) in the year 2000.

Even though he suffered badly from his mental health issues there was always a quip, even in death. When his fellow 'Goon', Sir Harry Secombe died from cancer, Spike commented, "I'm glad he died before me because I don't want him singing at my funeral!"

15

We'll Call You

The day of the recording arrived. We were due at the BBC television studios on Oxford Road, Manchester, at around noon. We'd been told to bring several pairs of shirts and trousers with us but very little else. I don't mean we'd been told to arrive naked – no! I mean that we'd been given very little information as to what was going to happen. We all piled in a car at around 11am. and drove into the city centre. Everybody knew where the BBC studios were but none of us could actually direct our driver. After asking several people, Denis, our chosen driver for the day, decided to take things into his own hands and proceeded to drive up a couple of one way streets the wrong way. Although he broke several highway laws on the way, he managed to guide us to our destination. The one's amongst us who weren't nervous beforehand certainly were by the time we arrived.

We reached our destination but the entrance was blocked by a massively ponderous gateway to the side of the building that was staffed by a uniformed guard. He was extremely polite and, after checking that we weren't persona non grata, directed us to a designated parking spot in the underground car park, after the gate had slowly trickled open. Once inside, we then had to walk all the way back to the entrance, to ask him where we went from there.

Everybody grabbed what they could from the car and with instruments, clothing and other essentials like 'Uncle Joe's Mintballs' for the throat, we made our way to reception. If you don't know what 'Uncle Joes' are, I'll tell you later!

An extremely well mannered lady greeted us on arrival and asked us to wait in the foyer until someone arrived to take us through to Studio One. In fact, everybody we met on that first and subsequent days were a joy! They met us with a smile and were always friendly and courteous on every succeeding visit. We sat, open mouthed, as television stars chatted and joked all around us. This was a different world and at least for an hour or two, we were being allowed to join in the fun! At that particular time though, it didn't seem like fun. We were as nervous as one could possibly be in the circumstances.

We were eventually met by a young woman who guided us through the labyrinth that is the BBC, passing that bloke who reads the news, to the canteen on the second, or was it third, floor, saying hello to that comedian and bumping into the guy who talks sport on the radio on a Saturday afternoon.

"I'll come back for you when Terry's ready", called the girl as she scurried out.

"I'm dying of thirst!" shouts Denis.

"That's the woman who does the weather!" calls David.

"I'll have a cup of tea," announces Norman.

"Look who's over there! It's that bloke from that soap, talking to that newsreader. I can't remember his name."

"This food's cheap! It must be subsidised. Looks good though. Should we have a meal now or wait a bit?"

"Isn't that Terry Wheeler over there?"

Sure enough, it was Terry walking towards us with a pile of scripts in hand.

"Good afternoon gentlemen! Hope you're feeling well and looking forward to this evening? Would you mind if I joined you for a cup of coffee?"

"Please, be our guest. David's at the counter, he'll get you a cup, sugar, milk? He's our treasurer for the day. David! Can you get Terry a brew?"

"Right gents, let's get your names right first of all, then I'll tell you what's going to happen in the next few hours."

Terry Wheeler then explained what happens on a day of filming.

"We'll go down to the studio in a couple of minutes. You'll need your guitars but you don't need to get changed at the moment. We'll run through the numbers a couple of times with Richie, our musical director and the lighting guy can tweak a few things. I'll be up in the box with our sound chappie. If you need anything, speak to Peter, the floor manager, he's in charge down there!"

So many people! So many things to get wrong! So many names to remember! And they've got a musical director! We're a folk group from Westhoughton – we don't need a musical director!

Instead of calming us down, Terry had definitely made us more nervous. We hurriedly finished our teas and coffees and with trepidation, excitement and a lot of expectation we took the lift down to Studio One.

"This is where they make 'A Question of Sport' and where the Halle orchestra record all their pieces."

Great, add a bit more tension to an already taut group of individuals! A smidgen of mental strain is all we need!

"Gentlemen, this is Richie Close, probably the best musician in Manchester!"

"Ow do lads!"

"You're not from round here are you?"

"No lads, I'm a 'Geordie' from Newcastle! They couldn't get a decent pianist in Manchester!"

Is he joking or does he really mean it?

"Don't worry lads, just a joke! Now what have you got for me today?"

Richie already knew what we were playing because it was in the script. In fact everything was in the script. Every word spoken by everybody who speaks, every camera angle, every lighting plot, every placement of every microphone and a margin to add more information should anyone need it.

"If you want to get your instruments and come into the side studio where the band are", suggests Richie.

We are led through a couple of double doors into a reasonably small room containing a band! There was a drummer, pianist (that's Richie), guitarist (no need for us then!), a woodwind player with an array of instruments and a keyboard player with an amazing assortment of keyboards.

"Let's start with the first song and we'll just follow you", said Richie.

The rest of the lads began to play and, what seemed like a full orchestra joined in the second bar of music! I noticed a few raised eyebrows amongst the musicians but Richie eased the tension by stating, "It's folk music lads! If that's the way they do it then that's the way we'll play it!" Pencils appear from everywhere as the musicians all alter their manuscripts.

"Just let's go through that again and we should be all right", retorts Richie.

"Well, at least it's more interesting than the last lot!" shouts another Geordie voice. It's the woodwind player who seems like a bit of a joker.

"Don't worry lads; we'll get it right after a few Carlsbergs!"

I noticed that there were microphones everywhere and a television screen in the corner. On the screen was what looked like a television "set" with an array of coloured scenery, curtains and a raised dais complete with several mike stands.

"That's where you're going next", chimed in the drummer, "you can't see the trapdoor from here!" All the musicians burst into laughter as Peter, the floor manager, arrived back in the room.

"Are we all sorted Richie? Terry's ready for them in the amphitheatre, I mean studio!" Another eruption of laughter exudes from the instrumentalists who thought it quite hilarious to frighten us all to death.

With tails between our legs we followed Peter from the room through another set of double doors, past lots of electrical wiring, pushing past several layers of black draping to exit onto a brightly lit television studio buzzing with activity. There were lighting engineers adjusting huge spotlights that completely obliterated the ceiling, four or five cameras with two engineers on each, men and women adjusting microphones, joiners with bits of wood and saws in their hands, other people moving chairs and scenery around when all of a sudden a booming voice cries, "Quiet down there! ..... Houghton Weavers please take your place on stage!"

Peter showed us where we would be standing on the platform. His job was to "manage" or co-ordinate all that is going on down there on the studio floor. He was answerable only to the producer, Terry Wheeler. To do this, he had an ear piece and a lapel microphone so he could communicate two ways with Terry in the production studio above. Everyone was scurrying around the studio floor with microphones, paint brushes, screw drivers etc....

Each member of the group had a microphone in front of them. I begin to move forward to adjust the height of my own mike. "Don't touch that!" boomed a voice from the studio floor, "that's the engineer's job!"

"I'm sorry", I begin, but a bloke came rushing forward and moved the offending instrument.

"You do the singing and I'll do my job! The unions will be on to you if you start doing that!"

But all I did was move a microphone about two inches!

Peter walked forward and smiled at me, "Don't worry Tony, they are union mad in here! Right boys, can we go through your two songs from beginning to end. Relax if you can, there's nothing to worry about until the audience arrives."

Audience, bloody audience! I'll have a heart attack before the audience arrives.

As we sang our two songs, people were rushing around adjusting lights, cameras and scenery. It would have been extremely interesting if I hadn't been so nervous. I noticed that the huge cameras seemed to float around the floor on a cushion of air. One was a massive machine with a crane-like arm that could go from side to side and up and down. It was another world! I just wished I hadn't been so anxious about everything.

"Right lads, take a break. The canteen's open upstairs, you know your way? I'll send someone to take you to make-up in about half an hour."

Peter then left us to our own devices as he approached a young woman who looked equally as nervous as ourselves. "Come this way please, would you take your place on stage. Terry, are you ready?" And so the juggernaut rolls on as the next "Christian" arrived in the arena.

We were buzzing with excitement as we made our way up to the restaurant.

"Did you see that bloke's guitar?" comments Norman. "What about that camera, it was amazing?" retorts Denis. "That girl who did the lighting was alright!" Trust David! All I could say was, "Where's the bar?"

20

It was a cacophony of noise, excitement, enthusiasm and sheer enjoyment! We could relax for a few minutes and enjoy the new experience of being part of it all. Everything in the studio was new to us. This was 1978 and mobile phones didn't exist, well not to ordinary folk like us. We didn't have a video recorder to record the shows because they were in their infancy and completely out of our price range. And forget the internet and personal computers – they were not to be seen for many years to come.

Showtime

We'd hardly time to eat our meal as we all wanted to talk at the same time and express our feelings about this new world. It was so exiting and we all wanted to take it in without forgetting that, at that moment, we hadn't yet done anything. We talked to an Irish guy dressed in an amazingly gaudy green suit who was performing on the same show. He'd done television in Ireland before and tried to reassure us that everyone was on our side whether we thought so or not. He told lots of gags to gauge their wittiness. I think we laughed through nervousness rather than anything else.

Next person to arrive at our table introduced herself as the floor manager's assistant. A floor manager's assistant is basically a "gopher".....will you gopher this or gopher that! She'd been asked to "gopher" the Houghton Weavers and take them to make-up. Once more down the rabbit warren of corridors that is the "beeb". We eventually arrived at a long room that looked exactly like a hairdressers. There were about six barber's chairs, each facing a large mirror that had light bulbs surrounding the frame. We were greeted by an extremely effeminate couple of blokes who introduced themselves as Paul and Victor.

"Ooh!" effused Victor, "I'll make you look like film stars. Which one wants me?"

"They're too butch for me!" replies Paul, "But I'll soon make them look like real men!"

"I'll have you!" states Victor, pointing to me, "Come and sit in my chair!"

"Ooh! You always liked the tall ones."

"I like them all as long as they can cope with me! Now what do you do, sweetie?" continues Victor.

"We sing in a group," was my reply.

"Ooh, doesn't he talk funny! Where are you from boys?"

"Westhoughton," I reply in the deepest voice I could conjure up.

"Don't worry about us guys, we're together and nothing is going to split us up!"

Openly gay relationships were very rare in the mid to late 70s. Acknowledgement and acceptance of those relationships took even longer to become customary. Although same sex relationships were established in law in 1967 in England, it was 1981 before the same could be said for Scotland and as recently as 2005 before civil partnerships became accepted in law in both those countries. In 2011 the United Nations passed its first resolution recognising gay and lesbian rights. This was followed by a report documenting violations of gay and lesbian people, including hate crimes, criminalisation of homosexuality and discrimination.

The one thing that Victor and Paul did that afternoon was to make us all laugh and forget about what was about to happen. They relaxed us all and were to become very good friends in the future.

So, wearing our new clothes, namely jeans and matching shirts; I seem to remember they were pastel shades of blue, green, red and yellow and sporting our hair and make-up, courtesy of Paul and Victor, we made our way to the television studio. Nothing could go wrong – we'd rehearsed it umpteen times! Glancing around at my colleagues I had the distinct feeling that they didn't concur with my sentiments. Although their faces were covered completely in greasepaint, cosmetics and probably sand and cement, it was obvious that all blood had drained from their faces and they appeared to be approaching the gallows!

For several minutes we were obliged to wait in the corridor outside the studio, whilst the preceding act went through their routine. It was greeted by rapturous applause which allayed some of our fears. All the acts this evening would have an entourage of family and friends, cheering them on. We were no exception to that rule, although we hadn't seen anyone apart from BBC staff. I knew that my mother, sister and brother would be waiting inside to cheer on their brother or son. The moment of truth was upon us as the doors were flung open and a voice from the ether asked the audience to, "Please welcome, The Houghton Weavers!"

From the dark of the corridor, we were plunged into astonishing illumination! The 'set' was brilliantly lit and as we walked towards our places, we were to experience completely different emotions. All were nervous and excited at the same time but whereas a couple of us nearly fell apart from feelings of dread and apprehension, the others were elated with a feeling of soaring expectation. I was in the latter camp and felt that this would be an experience that might never happen again, so it was up to me to make the most of it and perform to the utmost of my abilities! We were singing two songs so let's do the best we could. No introductions, no jokes, we just sang and played!

Our floor manager, Peter, coached the audience to break into applause, then slowly he turned to us, pointed towards David's guitar and it was off we go! I could hear Norman, Denis and David playing, but there was also the addition of another six musicians who were playing in the adjacent room. It sounds fabulous and I was singing along for around a minute when, all of a sudden, the backing band stopped playing, cameras turned away and, from the upstairs studio where the producer watched monitors that oversaw everything, a voice boomed over the tannoy, "Let's try that again please!"

What had I done! Did I sing the wrong words? Was I out of tune? Was I not looking into the right camera?

"Sorry everyone!" echoes the voice from above, "My fault! Let's start at the beginning!"

Phew, it wasn't my fault! But there were so many things to get right at the same time, it's a wonder that anything got done.

So we went through the whole rigmarole again. The second time it worked to perfection and the audience seemed as relieved as ourselves as they burst into rapturous applause. The next song was a doddle and it was over before I'd time to think. Peter, the floor manager thanked us and the crowd relaxed as they waited for the next participant. We left the

24

studio and walked to our dressing room. All was quiet and nobody knew what to say - I think we were all suffering from shock! We felt dejected as we were not needed anymore.

So that's what television was like!

We returned to our changing room and sat quietly in our own space. My mind was in a whirl but I didn't know how to vocalise my feelings. Eventually, we began to thaw and that's when it was difficult to get a word in. Everyone wanted to have their say and no-one wanted to wait enough to listen. We were talking whilst we were washing the make-up off our faces, making a dreadful mess in the room. Off came the stage clothes and it was into our best suits! We'd a reception to go to, where everyone would discuss the events of the evening. We could have a bite to eat and hopefully a beer or two!

"Well! what did you think?" piped up Denis, "I thought it was great!""

"So did I!" reiterates his brother.

"I nearly died when he stopped that first song," I chirped in, "I thought it was my fault."

"Well that's it gents!" piped in Norman, "the first of many more to come.......hopefully?"

"Let's go and see what they have to say. Is this Green Room far?"

Green Room

Following the show all acts and their managers were invited to the "Green Room" for a few nibbles and a glass of wine. Every theatre has a "Green Room" and I've often wondered why? After research I realise that I shouldn't have bothered as there are lots of reasons and nobody knows which is correct.

In Medieval times the actors usually performed outside on the green. In some London theatres the actual stage is still referred to as the "green". Therefore, the "Green Room" was considered to be the transitional room, as the actors made their way to the stage or the green. Years later, a green floor cloth was always spread on the floor of the stage for Tragedies. During the Reformation, however, most performances were Comedies and so the green floor covering was stored in the actors waiting room or lounge, hence "green" room.

It is said that the actors waiting room should be painted green to relieve the eyes from the glare of the stage. Some say that the main actors would be on the stage whilst the less experienced, or "green" performers would wait in a lounge adjacent to the performing area. In Shakespearean times, actors would prepare for their performances in a room filled with plants in the belief that the moisture from these shrubs would be beneficial to an actors voice, thus, "Green Room".

My favourite explanation however is the belief that many performers, including myself, suffer from nervous anxiety before a performance. As the person who feels sick is said to "go green" so the "Green Room" is the place where nervous actors would meet. There are many more explanations for this name but the real reason, or maybe a combination of reasons, have been lost in time. Whatever the reason, nearly every theatre in the country has a "Green Room" so it's up to you which description you choose.

So this particular "Green Room" was one of the meeting rooms that were adjoining the main TV studio. By the time we got there it was buzzing with a cacophony of sound. The Producer, Terry, was in conversation with Ray, who was the Managing Director of the BBC in Manchester. Musicians, stage crew, lighting engineers and camera operators were all mingling together....the musicians seemed to be the ones standing near the bar! All the acts that had performed that evening were nervously huddled together with their managers and agents. We didn't have a manager at the time and so we decided to join the musicians from the backing band. Well I did say they were near the bar!

"Well done lads", said Richie, their musical director, "Did you enjoy yourselves?"

"I think I would have enjoyed it more if I'd been less nervous", I counter.

"The more you do it, the more relaxed you become." Chance would be a fine thing! I said to myself. "Well, given the opportunity, I'd love to try it again", I said.

For the next half an hour or so, we made small talk with several people in the room. None of us wanted to leave as we felt that this was the life for us!

Enjoy it while you can, there may not be another chance!

As we prepared to leave Terry Wheeler approached us and said, "Well done gentlemen. I think it worked very well indeed. I may need your services again in the future...........speak to you over the phone!"

Need us again in the future. Does he really mean that or does he say that to everyone! I hoped not! I'm sure we would have loved to do that again and again! We'll see! We had to forget about it for that moment.......It was work the next day!

Mistakes

I overheard Terry talking to one of the other participants in the show.

"Yes, you'll need to come back next week but don't forget to bring the same dress!"

"What's that all about?" I asked one of the crew.

"Terry got a few camera angles wrong so he wants to shoot it again. There's not enough time tonight so he wants her in next week."

"Shouldn't be a problem, should it?"

"Not if she brings in the same dress!"

"What do you mean?"

"Continuity! If she sings two songs wearing two different dresses then people will ask questions."

"Does it matter?"

"You'd be surprised. Some people sit at home and all they do is look for mistakes! Do you not remember when that Boeing jet was seen in the sky during the chariot race in 'Ben Hur'?"

One of the earliest continuity errors seen on film was during the 1914 Charlie Chaplin film, 'The Property Man' where Chaplin emerges from one room bare headed but is seen in the very next clip, walking into the next room with his hat firmly on his bonce!

You'll find it all the time! One scene, the bloke is in the pub with about an inch of beer in his glass and the same scene, from a different angle, shows the pint pot full to the brim. The Marx brothers actually used a continuity error for comical effect in the film 'Duck Soup'. Groucho is seen with a hat on his head, next clip the hat has changed to a Napoleonic helmet, followed by a Prussian bearskin and so it went on!

"So if she doesn't bring the same dress, what will happen?"

"She'll not see herself on telly, unfortunately."

And that's exactly what happened! We heard several weeks later that the young woman thought she'd be smart and wear a different dress but Terry wouldn't have it and she was erased from the show.

To fill in the gap left by her omission Terry, the producer, filled it with clips from a previous artist. He was the Irish comedian we'd met earlier and told this long, rambling story but unfortunately he got it wrong, so he did it again and again, until eventually he got a roar of laughter when the 'punch line' worked!

We loved making mistakes because it could spawn lots of humour and we asked Terry much later, that if it ever happened to us, he should keep the cameras 'rolling' to see what might happen. Unfortunately he was to take absolutely no notice of our request!

Uncle Joe's Mintballs

Invariably, if I ever mention this delicacy, someone always asks me what it is. Well, I'll try and explain! William Santus was born in 1898 as one of seven brothers and sisters. He left school around the age of fourteen and worked on a fruit stall on Wigan market. Eventually he purchased his own stall selling fruit and vegetables. He met Ellen Seddon, who had been taught to make sweets by a friend and they began courting. William added a few bags of sweets to his stall as a sideline. Eventually the sweets took over!

Ellen and William were married in the Greenough Methodist church in Wigan. This church was the only building in Wigan that was bombed by the Germans during the Second World War Now is that a coincidence or an omen to would be couples?

I was told that a woman marries a man expecting him to change but he doesn't. Conversely, a man marries a woman expecting that she won't change and she does! Another one; when men talk to each other they constantly call each other names but don't mean a word of it. When women have a chat however, they complement each other all the time and equally don't mean a word of it!

Getting back to William and Ellen; by the end of the first decade of the Twentieth century they had sweet stalls in Wigan, Bolton and St. Helens. He eventually built a factory to make his sweets, only employing Methodists who were known by the current workforce, in order to keep a happy staff. Try doing that nowadays!

I heard one the other day! Some religious facts; Jews do not recognise Jesus as the Messiah; Anglicans do not recognise the Pope as leader of the Christian church and Methodists do not recognise each other in an off licence!

Uncle Joe's were not the only sweet made by Santus' but became the flagship of the company and was officially patented in 1933. William worked at the factory until his death in 1954 and was known to everyone as 'Uncle Joe'.

I've tried every remedy known to man to get rid of a sore throat. From obnoxious medicines to quite pleasant alcoholic concoctions but I've found that an Uncle Joes Mintball is the best ever remedy.

Uncle Joe's have been sighted at the top of mountains in India, villages in Kenya, Vancouver in Canada and even in the darkest depths of New York, USA! The pure goodness of Uncle Joe's Mint Balls is celebrated worldwide.

Work

As I related earlier, at the time I was working as an instructor of adults with learning difficulties. I worked in the Special Care unit which meant that the "trainees", as they were so called, were both physically and mentally impaired. It's not a job that everybody would do but I absolutely loved it. Nearly everyone walked around with a smile on their faces. The atmosphere was incredibly positive and both students and staff interacted constructively and encouragingly. There are moments in that type of occupation that will live with you forever and I'll try to explain a couple without giving too much away.

I'd said in the last few sentences how nearly everyone had a smile on their face. One particular trainee didn't see the lighter side of life and spent most of the time on the floor where she would spit and bite anyone who came near. Although she had the capability of speech no-one had ever heard her utter a word for several years. I spent a lot of time on the floor with her in an attempt to encourage her to vocalise. For my efforts I was bitten on several occasions and spat at regularly. Undaunted, we continued our strange relationship until one day, after several weeks, maybe months, I was about to stand up when she looked me straight in the eye and shouted "Hiya Pal!" Everyone in the room turned and there were several whoops of delight. From that moment onwards she began to speak more regularly. This is just a small example of how your day can turn from a mundane affair into total exhilaration. People were running around the workplace to tell as many people as were interested that she had spoken for the first time in years. Many years later I visited the centre and was greeted with "Hiya Pal!" from my friend, which caused me to blubber for several minutes!

Another occurrence happened whilst we were on a trip to Cornwall. In attendance were around a dozen students and almost as many staff. We had booked accommodation in a hotel for the week and during our stay we visited lots of places of interest including Lands End where we all posed for photographs and found out that Cape Town and New York were so many thousand miles away! One of the party was a particular pleasant gentleman from Bolton. He lived at home with his mother and was loved by everyone as he had a wonderful disposition. Although he had little vocabulary he could always communicate his needs. On the Friday afternoon before our departure the following day, he flew into a rage which was unheard of. He was banging tables and knocking over chairs so members of staff tried to ease his worries.

"Don't worry! We'll be going home tomorrow!"

"No we won't!" he replied, "I'm not going home!"

Staff members counteracted with, "Your mum's waiting for you. You'll see her tomorrow!"

"No I won't! No mum, no going home!"

Eventually he was calmed and in due course was tucked up in bed. We all had a chat to somehow explain his behaviour but it was difficult to clarify. The following morning at breakfast we had the same furore as the previous night. We all tried to make clear that we would be on our way home in a few hours time but were met with the torrent. "I'm not going home, no mum, no home!"

This inexplicable behaviour from someone normally so calm, was made clear within the hour. Our manager gathered all his staff in the dining room to explain that he'd had a phone call. The gentleman's mum had had a heart attack the previous evening at around the time of the disruption and she had died a few hours ago about breakfast time! We were all utterly shocked because I am convinced he knew! He never did go home and he never saw his mum again.

At times things can get quite difficult. During a training spell, I was working in a residential home for around 20 adults. I'd been grilled by the boss as to what I should and shouldn't do and warned by him about several of the residents.

"Whatever you do Tony, never find yourself alone with Jennifer (not her real name) because she has a tendency to shout 'rape' when left alone with a male member of staff."

"That could get to be quite difficult at times," I replied.

"Difficult or not, don't let it happen otherwise you could end up in serious trouble. It would mean the end of your job and your reputation!"

That was the end of that for quite a few weeks until I was asked if I could escort a group of adults to the cinema. It was about half a mile into town so we decided that on such a pleasant evening we should walk. Nothing of consequence happened until our journey home. Everyone was buzzing about the film and we were all in a tremendous mood. Jennifer was at the head of the party and I saw her disappear behind a huge advertisement hoarding. Not thinking that anything was amiss we were approaching the facade when I heard a friendly voice.

"Mr. Berry, can you come and help me please?"

It was Jennifer who was calling from behind the advert.

"Come out and tell me what you want." "Why don't you come here Mr. Berry and I'll show you!"

Immediately, I was filled with panic! What should I do? I daren't go behind the hoarding alone and she didn't seem to want to come out.

"Mr. Berry, Mr. Berry, come here and help me. I've got something to show you."

"Please come out Jennifer and you can tell me what you want."

"I want you to come here whilst I show you something!"

Then a flash of inspiration hit me. "I wonder what Jennifer wants? Should we all go and have a look?"

So more than a dozen people, with me in their midst, go around the back of the advertisement hoarding to find Jennifer lifting her dress up above her waist!

"What are you doing Jennifer?" asked one of the women.

"She's being stupid again!" retorted Billy.

"Pull your dress down and come out of there!"cried Angela.

I decided to join in, "Is everything okay Jennifer or do you want to show me something now?"

"No, it's okay Mr. Berry, I'm ready to go!"

I breathe a massive sigh of relief and thanked the stars that the boss had warned me about situations one should not find themselves in.

Jennifer could have been extremely troublesome but there were times when I had to laugh at her antics. The home where she lived was very close to Bolton Royal Hospital. If Jennifer had a night out on the town, she had a tendency to collapse at 'home time'. She was either having an epileptic fit or a heart attack (I don't think she actually ever had either). The landlord of the pub saw this disabled girl writhing on the floor in agony and so called the emergency services and an ambulance duly arrived. Jennifer was strapped into a stretcher and gently hoisted into the waiting vehicle. As the van pulled up in front of the Accident and Emergency entrance to the hospital, Jennifer would step out of the ambulance with a smile on her face, bid everyone 'thank you and goodnight' and walk just round the corner to her accommodation! Who needs to spend money on a taxi!

Working with adults with learning difficulties isn't for everyone but for the people who work in that profession there are precious moments that will live forever in the memory. I have made countless friends with both students and staff and I am very much richer from those experiences.

Gigs

Although we'd recorded the television show, it hadn't yet been screened, so we were still doing small shows in even smaller venues. Most bookings are done six months or so before the actual date so things take a while to trickle through. I distinctly remember a night in Wrightington, near Wigan, when we appeared at the village hall. The show was going quite well as we approached the interval. Norman was explaining that supper of pie and peas (well it had to be pies in Wigan!) would be collected from upstairs, so if everyone would make their way towards this door, go up the stairs, collect their supper and come down the stairs at the other side of the room.

"Just a minute!" shouts the organiser, "Tell 'em they can only go up four at a time!"

"What do you mean?" we ask.

"Well the joists in the ceiling have got woodworm and we daren't allow more than four up in case the roof collapses!"

On another occasion we were preparing for the interval, during which supper would be served. We had one more song to go before the break and we explained the routine for collecting their repast. Off we went with the final song in the first half. We ended the song to a round of applause when the organiser popped her head around the door jamb.

"Would you please sing one more?"

"Not a problem....for our last song in the first half........here we go"

We ended the song to another ovation when the same head popped through the opening.

"You couldn't possibly sing another one please?"

"Ladies and gentlemen, for our final song in the first half...." To much humour and gossip we began. At the end of the song it happened a third time, "Please.....just one more!"

"We can do twenty more if you need us to but why do you keep letting us do the last one then ask for another?"

"Well, you don't understand!"

"I know we don't understand but we would if you explained!"

"Well, as you know we're having pie and peas."

"Yes, we know, but that's not clarified the problem!" we responded.

"And we're making the pies in our kitchens."

"What's the bloody problem, missus?"

"Well the pie's done but the crust isn't brown yet, so could you do one more!"

You couldn't make these stories up! Something generally happened every night. From dressing rooms that were glorified cupboards to stages that were held together with bits of string. All of them add to the rich tapestry that is the life of an entertainer!

Sit Thi Deawn

Within a month of our first appearance on television, Terry Wheeler rang to say that everyone had enjoyed our performance on "We'll Call You" and asked if we possibly knew around 30 songs. If so, he'd like to invite us down to sing on a new series that he had been working on.

"Of course, Terry, we know hundreds of songs."

Because we'd had three or four folk clubs on the go for the last few years it had necessitated us learning several songs every week so that our repertoire wouldn't get stale. We had guests from around the folk world and picked up tips from them. We'd like to think we kept the best bits and discarded the worst.

"My idea is that you'd sing a few songs every week and Stu Francis and Joe Gladwin would entertain in their own inimitable way!" Stu, a Bolton lad, was to gain fame through Granada TV's 'The Comedians' and as the host of BBC's 'Crackerjack' where he coined his catchphrase, 'I'm so excited, I could crush a grape!'

Joe Gladwin, on the other hand, was an established star as Stan Hardman, driver for Nelly Pledge's Pickle factory in 'Nearest and Dearest'. He was Fred Jackson, owner of the local fish and chip shop in 'Coronation Street' and famously, as the long suffering husband of Nora Batty in 'Last of the Summer Wine'. Many people will recognise his dulcet tones as the voice of the 'Hovis' ad for many years. Joe himself, I would think, would rather be remembered as a knight of the papal order of St. Gregory for his services to the church and his community.

The Pontifical Equestrian Order of St. Gregory the Great was established in 1831 by Pope Gregory XVI and some notable beneficiaries of the order include Sir Alex Ferguson, Sir Henry Cooper, Sir Matt Busby and Frank Carson.

Stu and Joe were to partake in a sketch every week, where the youngster (Stu) would extol the virtues of the present whilst the old guy (Joe) would tell him that things were far better in the "olden days". Stu would generally have the better argument but invariably Joe always came out the winner!

So we arrived on the allotted day to prepare for a show that would give us some regular television exposure. It wasn't until we arrived at the studios in Oxford Road, Manchester and began running through the show that we realised it was OUR show. We all had the impression that we were guests on someone else's programme until we started to read the script and the title of the series, "Sit Thi Deawn" which is the title of one of our favourite tunes, telling of the hospitality of a Lancashire household. Sit down and make yourself at home it says and here we are, in the BBC and they're calling a show after the title of one of our songs. It really was hard to take in!

The show ran on similar lines to our previous visit, the difference being was, we were the main act! So the cameras, the make-up, the sound people and everyone else for that matter were there just for us! There was an audience of around 200 people cheering us on, together with family and friends we'd invited along. We arrived at lunch time to run through the show several times for everyone's benefit, including ourselves. We renewed acquaintances with cameramen, stage hands, floor managers, make-up and the backing band and slowly began to relax as we ran through the first show in the series.

During lunch break I bumped into Ray, the M.D. at BBC NorthWest.

"How's everything going Tony?"

"Fine, I think. Once we get used to everything I'm sure we'll be okay."

"Is there anything you need?"

"Well, since you ask", I replied, "When we're in the TV studio, it gets very hot and I wouldn't mind a drink?"

"You mean tea or coffee? I'm afraid it's not allowed in the studio because the liquid can damage the floor if it's spilt."

"No, I was thinking more like beer! And I promise you it won't get spilt! If any is, I'm usually underneath it before it hits the floor!

The floor manager's assistant said we couldn't have drinks for the same reason you gave, but you did ask!"

Ray smiled and said, "I'm the boss around here! Just leave it to me!"

With that little obstacle sorted out we got down to work. When you prepare a show it takes several hours of gruelling rehearsals before everyone is satisfied with what they have to do. From camera angle, lighting plots to sound balance, appropriate clothing and make-up. This all took place from around noon until approximately 6pm. There was only time for a short tea break then it was down to make-up and into the studio for the half hour show which took around two hours to record.

So we'd rehearsed the show thoroughly, had something to eat and been to see our friends in make-up, to get rid of any little blemishes, or big blemishes when it came to me! I found it rather fascinating; they'd put some green stuff on my face as a sort of undercoat, then a beige covering so that all our faces were the same colour and texture. All our clothes had been re-ironed to make them perfect and we looked like tailors dummies as we approached the double doors leading into the recording studio.

Inside the studio is a "warm up" man. As the BBC would like to put it:

He is known to stars and producers alike. He has featured in loads of hit TV shows. He doesn't win awards, go to celebrity parties or feature in Heat Magazine. He has to make people laugh who want to see someone else. He is the warm up man.

And that is exactly his role – to relax the audience so that they begin to think they are in a theatre or at home listening to a favourite of theirs, especially when a large percentage of the audience is a friend or family. I can only liken it to a sporting event, when parents and friends are probably more tense than the competitors.

They'll say things like, "If you're sitting with someone you shouldn't be with, now's the time to change places", or, "I don't think I need to tell you where the fire exits are. We're never going to have two fires in a week!"

Once relaxed, the audience is left in the capable hands of the 'floor manager'. He tells everyone when to clap, when to keep quiet, when to laugh or cry, whether you want to or not. He'll rehearse the crowd for a few minutes then it's down to us!

"Ladies and gentlemen, please welcome the ones you've all come here to see, The Houghton Weavers." At which point we would burst through the doors and try to remain as calm as possible, which wasn't easy when there were a couple of hundred people watching our every move? "We've done this before, gents, but this time it's all ours, so let's have a good time ....'break a leg'".

Now that's a phrase you've probably heard before, however, the meaning of it is somewhat obscure. Actor's wishing someone 'good luck' would probably give them bad luck so they used the phrase 'break a leg'. In Greek plays the audience were said to stamp their feet if they approved. If they stamped too much they could 'break a leg'. Similarly, banging the chair you were sitting on, in appreciation of a performance, could easily 'break a leg'. In Shakespearian times to 'break a leg' was to bend the knee when taking a bow but I'm going to go for a more recent explanation. During the times of Vaudeville, each act only performed for a few minutes each. The theatre managers, to cover themselves, regularly booked more acts than were necessary, just in case. Unfortunately, the acts only got paid if they actually appeared on stage. That happened if they passed the imaginary line of curtains (or legs) that surrounded the stage, therefore 'breaking the leg' in order to get paid.

I think I'll stick with the dancer's choice of phrase before they walk on stage. Rather than break a leg, they all say to each other "Merde!" (You'll need a French/English dictionary if you don't know what that means!)

So here we are, on stage at the BBC, singing our songs, for our show....unbelievable! And sure enough, true to his word,

Ray has made sure that there are pints of bitter hidden behind every piece of scenery, for all of us to quench our thirst!

The two hours flew by and it was back to the dressing room to wash off the make-up and down to the Green Room for a chat with our relatives who had been allowed to stay back for a sandwich and a drink. Everyone was tremendously excited and exuberant in their praise. Terry, the producer, introduced himself to everyone and then went on walkabouts, congratulating all his staff.

For a few minutes, the talk was all about the show we'd just recorded, then just as quickly, it was back to the weather and football. Back to mundane reality where the only concerns were the bank balance, whether the lawn needed mowing, or should I get my hair cut? I began to realise that, for them, it's just another day at work! I hoped that I would never feel that doing what I did was just another day at work!

It was early last December, as near as I remember,
I was walking down the street in tipsy pride;
No one was I disturbing, as I lay down by the curbing,
A pig came up and lay down by my side.
As I lay there in the gutter, thinking thoughts I shouldn't utter,
A lady passing by was heard to say; '
You can tell a man who boozes, by the company he chooses",
And the pig got up and slowly walked away!

Anon
The Oxford Book of light American Verse 1979

42

Red Lion

At that time, my local in Westhoughton was the Red lion. I'd go there for a drink and a chat with my mates. We'd have a game of darts and the place, unlike the pubs of today, buzzed with excitement. There was a folk club upstairs on a Friday which I attended regularly. Bowlers from the Crown Green 'panel' filled one corner of the bar chatting about their exploits on the turf. The local Amateur dramatic society sometimes held their meetings in one of the small rooms, as did the Rotary Club. There were football teams, netball teams, rounder's teams and darts teams who used the premises as their headquarters. When everybody found out that we were due to be on television there was a genuine affection from the regulars. The pub was a bit of a warren of many small rooms where different factions of the community regularly gathered. One such room was a television lounge just off from the bar area. It was quite unusual in those days to see a television in a pub. You went to the alehouse to get away from the telly!

Our programme was being screened on a Friday evening at around 10pm. During that era few people would sit and watch television in a drinking establishment but this was different! This was a local lad and we all knew each other so it was important! As we neared the bewitching hour the room began to get full and my friend John, was sitting in the front row. Behind him sat Tommy Gorringe one of the hardest men in town. As a voice using the Queen's English began...........

"And now ladies and gentlemen please sit back and listen to ....The Houghton Weaver!"

Over the airwaves come the dulcet tones of yours truly...........

"Aye mon I'm fain to see thi Sit Thi Deawn..............." John stands up walks over to the television and changes channels to Granada and proceeds to burst out laughing.

Without a word, from behind him appears the spectre of Tommy who, using both hands, changes the channel back to BBC1 with one hand and punches John in the face with the other!

"..............For ahm gradely fain to see thi Sit Thi deawn."

John is groaning in the corner of the room whilst mopping his bloodied nose and everyone is telling him to shut up and watch the programme!

John looks up through dazed eyes and says, "I'm sorry! I was only having a joke!"

Tommy says quietly, "Well go and have a joke somewhere else!"

So there I am, sitting with my mates, watching a television show that I'm in, with nobody taking any notice of me, just watching the telly! Great! That's what I want it to be like – no prima donnas allowed in Westhoughton!

As the programme reaches its conclusion, everyone retreats back to the bar and that's the end of that. I'm on quite a considerable 'high' whilst it's back to who we play next at darts, dominoes or bowls and whether Bolton will defeat the opposition at Burnden Park tomorrow! No mention of the programme we've just watched, it's back to reality! I daren't ask what they thought of the show as I know what their reply will be. I'll only find out tomorrow morning when my mother will give me the 'low down'!

Theatre Royal, St. Helens

And so we became television celebrities. Wherever I went for the next few weeks, people would comment that they'd seen us on telly. We were getting regular phone calls from agents and managers who were constantly asking if they could represent us. Bookings were coming in thick and fast from every type of venue, from the regular pubs and clubs we'd been doing, to theatres and bigger night clubs.

The first theatre to contact us was the Theatre Royal in St. Helens. The manager there had seen our first appearance on TV and so booked us to appear at his theatre. In the mid to late 70's most people attended social clubs and night clubs for their entertainment and lots of theatres had closed their doors for the last time. Many were dilapidated and seriously run down and it took the likes of theatre lovers, with the help of artists such as Ken Dodd, to keep these marvellous emporiums alive. The cost of restoring one of these such buildings is astronomical and the people raising money didn't have the "National Lottery" to aid them.

The Theatre Royal had the resources of the Pilkington family to help them. A local family, the Pilkington's built up the art of glass making to the point that St. Helens became the home of glassmaking. The Pilkington family started a glass company in 1826 and in 1894, Pilkington Brothers was founded. Glass is made by melting sand, limestone and other minerals such as dolomite. They would be drawn from the furnace in a molten state, rolled to the desired thickness, then polished on both sides. The family patented a new method in the 1950s, where molten glass is floated on molten tin. Molten tin is extremely smooth so that glass does not need to be polished making it a much cheaper process.

By the early 1990s the Pilkington's owned every glass manufacturing plant around the world, bar one, thus giving them an obvious monopoly. In 2006 they were taken over by the Japanese company N.S.G. They continue to innovate and have recently developed a self cleaning glass that breaks down dirt with sunlight which is then washed away with the rainfall. Great news for everyone except window cleaners!

In the 1960s the Theatre Royal was purchased by the Pilkington family for use by their employees and other local amateur dramatic societies. The building was gutted internally and completely refurbished, saving this grand old building for future generations. By the 1980s the company deemed it no longer appropriate to own a theatre and donated it to the local Council in 1986, who, in turn established a trust, to continue its work.

The manager of this great emporium saw us on our first television show and booked us to appear at his venue, making it our very first theatre gig. On the night of the show, it was obvious that our small sound rig would not be appropriate for such a large hall so we had to hire a company to provide us with amplification. Thus we came into contact with "Teddy" Lowton for the very first time. Teddy would arrive at the theatre several hours before the show, set up all the gear and wait for our arrival. A great character, who would have various helpers, to help carry all the sound equipment in and out of the venue. Teddy was loud, brash and wonderful. Everyone who came into contact with him fell in love with him and all his helpers. So many wonderful tales to tell, most of them unrepeatable, travelling the world with stars who needed his genius behind the sound desk. Another bloke who helped Teddy was Winston, who was a lighting engineer. He would help when he had a night off. His tales were even more unrepeatable than Teddy's! We all became firm friends and spent many years working together.

We had a fabulous night in St.Helens and still return there to this day!

Transition

It was quite a strange time really. We'd be working in a vast theatre one night, followed by a room in the back of a pub the following night! We loved the intimacy of a small audience and still do, but larger audiences mean larger fees, so common sense prevails. We'd already done a television series and Terry, the producer, was talking about a follow up one, so we had to think about our futures. We were all working full time and also working most nights of the week. We still ran three folk clubs during the week and were getting more and more bookings for the weekends.

It got to the point where I became quite ill. During that period, I was seconded, from work, to attend a one year course at Bolton College. The course work was well within my capabilities but attendance was very important. The boss of the course was a stickler for attendance, to the point where it seemed more important to him than the actual written work.

I was constantly on the toilet and felt extremely unwell. Following a few visits to my local G.P. I was referred to a specialist. I didn't think much about it until I got the letter, which gave me my allotted appointment. It was the same day that my sister had died several years previously and I was, by now, the same age as she was at the time! Panic stations! I've got cancer, I'm dying! Every scenario ran through my mind. Just as I'm beginning to do OK, I'm going to die!

My sister, Anne, had died several years before from as cerebral haemorrhage. This is caused by bleeding in the brain which causes intracranial pressure, which can lead to a coma, or in my sister's case, death. My whole family had been devastated by her passing and it took many years before I could discuss the event without bursting into tears. She was only twenty-eight and the regional midwife in our area.

For the next few weeks, I couldn't stop thinking about my problem, which was getting worse because of my nervousness. Eventually I went to see the specialist and he gave me several examinations, x-rays and the like. I was eventually diagnosed as having ulcerative colitis, which is a great thing to get if you need to lose weight! The problem was, I didn't need to lose weight! Although the ailment can become a problem I was overjoyed! It's curable and I'm going to be OK!

Unfortunately, I'd had some time off from college. Although I'd got a doctor's note to say that I was incapacitated at the time and unable to attend college, the boss sent for me!

"Do you realise that you've had several days off college!"

"Of course I do", was my reply, "but I've got a doctor's note to say that I was too unwell to attend."

"You can't be that unwell!"

"What do you mean?" was my reply.

"Well, I saw you on television last week and you didn't look ill to me!"

"Yes, but that was recorded weeks ago and make-up is a marvellous thing!" "Not my problem! I think I'm going to have to ask you to leave the course."

"But that's totally unfair! I'm up to date with the course work and I've a doctor's certificate to say that I wasn't well enough to attend college!"

"Still not my problem! Attendance on this course is of paramount importance and you've simply not been attending!" So that was that! I had to unceremoniously leave college with my tail between my legs, go back to work and try and explain myself.

They were very understanding and sympathised with my predicament, as most of them had attended the same college course. Unfortunately, it left me in somewhat of a dilemma, as I couldn't progress up the ladder of promotion without the certificate that came with the course.

It always makes me wonder why sick people have to go to the very back of a supermarket to get their prescriptions but smokers can get their cigs at the front door!

I suppose it made life easier when, a couple of months down the road; we had a meeting to decide our future.

"I don't know whether you realise it but we've got 17 bookings next month!"

"Well that's good isn't it?"

"It's very good but we are getting more by the day. We need to think about what we are going to do next."

"Like what?"

"Like whether we pack in work and just do the singing or whether we stay at work but cut down on the singing. We can't keep it up the way we are going, Tony's already been ill. We'll all be in the same boat if we don't do something about it!"

"You're quite right but we've all got decent jobs. Singing is a very precarious occupation."

"Yes, I know, but we'd only regret it if we didn't give it a whirl!"

For many weeks we contemplated the whys and wherefores of it all. Should we or shouldn't we make the move to full time singing with the group. Finally, it was decided that we would all leave work and try to make it in the very risky business that's called "show". Norman would pack in work earlier than everyone else and look after the bookings, until we could find someone with more knowledge to take care of the business side. We would all hand in our notices within the next couple of months and see if we can make a living as musicians.

So from then on we became full time musicians! I prefer 'full time' as opposed to 'professional'. I don't think I'll ever be that!

Manager

Following our appearance on television and with the information that we ran our own affairs, management agencies came knocking on our door. We would arrive at a theatre to find sandwiches, tea, coffee and a crate of beer in our changing rooms.

"They've been left by such and such an Agency," came the reply. "They'll call backstage later to have a chat!"

So for several months this type of thing happened and we met many executives from various theatrical agencies who required us to sign on the dotted line. Some were spookier than others. It wasn't as easy to find out about them as it is nowadays with the advent of the internet and various other resources. We had to take them at face value and decide whether we could trust our livelihoods to these impresarios! Some were small time whilst some were very big time! We eventually plumped for one more or less in the middle. He ran an agency that managed only a handful of acts which we preferred. We didn't like the idea of being a small fish in a very big pond, rather a larger fish in a smaller pond! Brian was a likeable bloke who wooed us with his honesty and professionalism. He managed several acts, the biggest at the time being the Dooley's, a family pop group consisting of two sisters two brothers and a drummer! They had several hits in this country but were absolutely massive in Japan. So much so, that they once toured Japan, using Michael Jackson as their warm-up act!

They were quite a cheesy act and certainly not followed by the young people who felt 'hip'. One wonderful story that I remember about them was related to an article in one of the pop magazines; I think it was NME? (New Musical Express). The editorial went roughly like this:

"I've had rather a traumatic week. Been to see several acts and at one of the concerts I inadvertently left my handbag! Besides money, plastic cards and make-up I had numerous tickets for up-coming shows featuring the biggest names in pop. Much to my delight I had a phone call to say that my handbag had been found. My delight turned to dismay when I found that the only thing left in the handbag were a pair of tickets for the Dooley's!"

So we now had a manager! We would go down to his office, which would be festooned with photographs of many famous people, just to have a chat and find out how things worked in this industry. Brian would make the important calls to television people and record companies etc. whilst several staff members would do the 'nitty gritty' of getting us work. Will we make it? Will it last more than a few months? Who can tell? But we'll make a damn good go of it. We might still be going when we're forty!

Besides getting us work, Brian tried very hard to find us sponsorship deals and a major recording contract. He was successful on both counts, securing an agreement with both Tetley brewery and Takamine guitars, together with a three year recording deal with E.M.I.

As they say, 'There's one great advantage in being a failure in show business; you never have to worry about making a comeback.'

'Knock, knock.'
'Who's there?'
'Kylie'
'Kylie who??'
'That's showbiz!'

Driving

Up until that time I had absolutely no interest in driving and took the bus, train, or cadged a lift from friends. We were in the middle of our second series of 'Sit Thi Deawn' and I felt it was time I bit the bullet and began driving. I'd contemplated it several times in the past but didn't have the urge or passion to continue but this was different. I was appearing on television but still catching the bus to go places!

So I went out and bought a battered old Mini 1000 which gave me the impetus to learn how to drive. I never had a lesson from a driving instructor but got my mates to sit in the car whilst I learned the ins and outs of driving a car. I immediately put in for my test and bought a copy of the Highway Code. Without any nerves whatsoever I took my test and failed miserably! I'd not done too badly but I always remember a question that I got wrong. The driving test officer showed me a sign showing three, two and one diagonal red stripes on a white background.

"What is this please?" he asked.

"Not a clue, sorry!"

Do you, the reader know? You'll find the answer on page 1,541; only joking! It's three, two and one hundred yards before a level crossing.................so now you know!

Several weeks later I took my test again and have never been as terrified of anything in my life. Much worse than going to the dentist! I was so nervous that after about ten minutes, the instructor asked me to stop the car. He then said, "Why don't you get out of the vehicle sir, have a walk round and try to relax?"

"Thanks very much but I think I'd like to get it out of the way!"

I shook all the way round the course but at the end of it all I was over the moon when he told me I'd passed!

Some months later, as I drove to Ormskirk, to record an episode of 'Surprisingly it's Spring' I was involved in an accident on the East Lancs. road and my mini was written off! Fortunately, no one was hurt and it wasn't my fault so that saved my insurance premium from going through the roof!

With the insurance money I put a deposit on a brand new MG sports car and became the biggest poser in town! I hope I didn't but I'm quite sure many folk in Westhoughton thought that I was!

Bloke comes home from work and is greeted by his wife,

"Hello dear, have you had a good day?"

"Well I've got some good news and some bad news, which would you like first?"

"I think you'd better give me the good news!"

"The good news is, the air bags work!"

A bloke came over to a chap in Westhoughton and said,

"Do you know the quickest way to Bolton, please?"

Bloke says, "Are you walking or driving?"

"Driving", comes the reply.

"Well that's definitely the quickest way!"

Alan Fawkes

One of the musicians who played during our TV shows was flautist, saxophonist, penny whistle player and general woodwind maestro, Alan Fawkes. He originated from the North East, South Shields to be precise and for many years to come was to become an honorary Weaver. Alan was a freelance musician who worked in many areas of the music business. He deputised on numerous, occasions for the Halle orchestra, did much work for the BBC and ran a jingles business called Alfasound.

A jingle is a short tune used in advertising and for many commercial uses. The jingle contains one or more hooks that explicitly promotes the product being advertised. [Wikipedia]

Alan's greatest love was jazz music and he played all over the world with various bands including his own. After several shows for the BBC we asked if he was available to back us on one or two shows. He became a permanent fixture for over 10 years! Alan had a very pronounced stutter which got worse as he got more frustrated. He used to comment, "At the end of our sssstreet, there's a sssschool for sssstutterers but I'm ssself taught!"

Alan started playing musical instruments after seeing Charlie Cairoli, the famous clown, playing an instrument he loved but did not recognise. It was similar to a clarinet but gold rather than black. Alan eventually found that it was a soprano saxophone. At the time, he was a plumber, working on an estate of newly built houses. He purchased a sax and proceeded to teach himself how to play. So that nobody could hear the squeaks, Alan decided to stay late at work and practise in the nearly completed houses where he was

54

working. Following several months of practise he could blow a tune but thought that if he wanted to become a musician he'd better learn how to read music. Also, if he wanted to work in a band, he'd need to be able to play in different keys. So, every tune he taught himself, he was able to play in every key, which to a musician is quite incredible! He then went for a lesson! Within five minutes with a teacher he realised that he knew far more than the teacher and so he became a player who regularly played in a world renowned orchestra (the Halle) being completely self taught! So I think we should thank Charlie Cairoli for bringing us Alan Fawkes!

Charlie Cairoli was born to a French circus family in Affori, Italy in 1910. He became a clown at the age of seven and travelled extensively, appearing with his father as part of a clown family. In 1939 he appeared at the Circus Krone in Munich, Germany. At a special performance, attended by Adolf Hitler, he was presented with a watch by the Fuhrer. When World War II broke out Charlie was appearing at the Tower Circus in Blackpool. As news of the war broke, the story goes that Charlie reputedly walked to the end of the North Pier and threw the watch into the sea!

He decided to stay in Blackpool after the war and became a permanent fixture, appearing a world record forty consecutive years at the same venue. He was a fixture on television during the 70's having his own children's show, "Right Charlie". His distinguishing feature, besides his one piece suit and bowler hat, was his red nose, many, many years before it was adopted as the emblem of the Comic Relief or "Red Nose" charity.

Back to Alan! He was well known for arriving very late at gigs, so we eventually got used to it. So much so, that we would go on stage at the allotted time, only to see Alan arrive a few minutes later, bag over his shoulder, walking onto stage playing his saxophone as though nothing had happened. We were once entertaining in a marquee and Alan, as usual, was fifteen minutes late. As we continued into our third song, he arrived and started playing outside the tent which startled a woman so much that she had an 'accident'. We arrived at a theatre in Northamptonshire one weekend, only to be told that Alan had arrived the previous week! He had walked into the theatre, asked where the Weavers were, was told it was next week and calmly walked out with bag over his shoulder.

Alan had a great love of limericks and two readily spring to mind:

There was a young girl from Dundee
Who got stung on the neck by a wasp
I said, "Did it hurt?" she said, "No not at all!"
"It can do it again if it likes!"
Or:
On the chest of a barmaid from Sale
Was tattooed all the prices of ale
And on her behind, for the sake of the blind,
Was the same information in Braille.

Frankie

If anyone in my stories ever deserves a chapter all to himself then it's Frankie. He's not actually called Frankie though, his real name is Keith. I grew up with him on the periphery of my circle of friends. His name used to bring the fear of God into my life. He was a very tough character who went to the Senior lad's school as opposed to my upbringing with the left-footers, or "catlicks" as they used to call us. Whenever the precipitation in Westhoughton became white, it was either due to snow or the occasional "fall out" from an erupting Daisy Hill volcano. The former usually heralded a mass snow fight between the "catlicks" and "proddies". At school dinner time (lunch to you), they'd stream over what is now the central park in Westhoughton, although it was then a rubbish dump. We'd be organising our forces on the "Alick", a hill close to our school. At the forefront of our clan would invariably be Tommy Gorringe who could make snowmen rather than snowballs with his huge fists. He'd be ably assisted by Jimmy Lally and certainly at least one member of the Roberts and Brigdale families. I didn't know the names of most of our assailants apart from big Stan and Keith. "Big" Stan, as his name implies, was huge and he pushed me around a bit as a youngster. He was quite frightening but I eventually found a pussycat beneath the bearlike frame. Keith would be near the front whilst Stan took close guard as far behind him as is possible, so as not to make him appear cowardly. We'd hurl snowballs into the air across King Street in the hope of hitting a target. We all felt like archers at the battle of Crecy.

Crecy was a battle where the leaders of each opposing side, namely the kings of France and England respectively, led their armies from the front. Well, just off the front, a bit like Stan! It was the battle that gave the archers of England and Wales their fame. Although we've used the bow since stone-age times, this was the time that it reached its zenith as the major weapon of warfare in this country. Fortunately, nobody else thought it was a good idea because it took years of practice to be proficient, so we were top of the pile when it came to fighting! It must have been a popular pastime in England and the poorer people practiced all the time. I suppose it was a way out of poverty like football or boxing is today – if you became proficient you could gain a certain respect amongst your peers. It is reported that many of the Welsh archers on their return to Wales were given an acre of land each and were granted "freeman" status, which made then exempt from paying taxes for grazing their cattle.

So here we have the English, who've decided they'll invade France, on their way home via Calais, when they are ambushed by the French at Crecy. The English have between nine and ten thousand troops depending on your source, whilst the French have between thirty six and one hundred thousand, again depending on source. The English who are outnumbered by, at the very minimum, three to one decide to stop and fight. They are led by Edward III and his sixteen year old son, Edward, who was later to be nicknamed the Black Prince. At one point the king is asked if his son should be given help on the battlefield and "daddy" says, "I am confident he will repel the enemy without my help - let the boy win his spurs!" – treated 'em hard in those days!

The arrogant French decide that this battle is going to be "easy peasy" so they send in their mercenary Genoese crossbowmen to sort out the English. Unfortunately, they can only send one of their bolts every two minutes, whereas the archers can release an arrow every five seconds. Following wave after wave of arrows the Genoese decide they've had enough after a few short minutes and decide to run. Their French bosses think they are cowards and start to slaughter them on the battlefield. This jams up the whole thing and they get stuck in the mud and the dead bodies of their so-called allies! The archers continue to rain arrows on the knights and completely decimate them. The French apparently tried sixteen charges, all were unsuccessful and they suffered devastating losses. The English losses were in their hundreds whilst the French were reported to have lost as many as 30 thousand. The majority of French aristocracy were either killed or captured on the battlefield and it took many years before they recovered. One of the aristocracy was the king of Bohemia. He was almost blind but rather than back down, he tied his horse to other knights so that he could be led into battle. The Black Prince was so impressed by his bravery, that he took his feathers and slogan as his own. The three feathers and the motto 'Ich Dien' have belonged to the Prince of Wales ever since.

I'll leave the last words on this battle to the French chronicler Froissant who described the action thus.....

"Once the English formation was within crossbow range the Genoese discharged their bolts; but the rain had loosed the strings of their weapons and the shots fell short. The English archers each stepped forth one pace. Drew the bowstring to his ear and let their arrows fly; so thick that it seemed as snow....."

So here we are, hurling snowballs at each other for about half an hour, fingers getting more and more numb until, eventually, the school bell goes and we all return to class to blow life into our paralysed limbs. I remember, we would put the frozen bottle of milk on the radiator and by the time we returned to them, the milk was beautifully warm! On those days I used to fear the journey home, hoping and praying that I wouldn't meet Frankie and Stan on Church Street.

As we grew older we eventually became friends and regularly met in the pub for a few pints and a game of darts. It was in the Wheatsheaf where he was to gain his infamy and his nickname! One of the most popular shows on television during the late 60's and early 70's was "Please Sir" telling of the exploits of newly qualified teacher, Bernard Hedges, played by John Alderton and the class of 5C in Fenn Street School. One of the pupils was Frankie Abbott, played by David Barry. His name was to live on! When we went out to Bolton night clubs at weekends, we'd invariably try to chat up a girl. If one wasn't too sure what she'd look like when one was sober, it was usual to use a pseudonym or alias!

So here we are, sat at the bar of the Wheatsheaf, when in walks a stranger. She walks up to the bar and asks, "Is Frankie in?"

"Frankie? I'm sorry love but I don't know anyone by that name," replies the barman.

So the girl orders a drink and continues asking the whereabouts of Frankie Abbott. Everyone answers in the negative. Nobody knows anyone who comes in this pub called Frankie. The girl decides to finish her drink before leaving for home, following her fruitless journey to Westhoughton, when the doors of the pub burst open and in walks Keith.

"Oh, Frankie, you're here at last!" cries the girl, "Nobody in the pub knew you!"

"Frankie!" comes the unanimous chorus from everyone round the bar. And that was how it came to pass!

Everyone who comes to know Frankie, realises that he's a truly genuine character and is always game for a laugh. I played darts with him, visited night clubs with him, drank with him and eventually went on holiday with him! We decided that the South of France would be a place where he could express himself. He'd been there the previous year with another friend of mine and tales of their exploits became legendary!

During the preceding year, Frankie had been on holiday with Jamesy (real name, Steve) and on their first night in the area had ventured to the principality of Monaco to look in at the casino in Monte Carlo. Frankie was given the dubious honour of being banker for the evening, so all that the two possessed was in a money belt round his waist. Steve had taken several francs (the currency at the time) and wandered off round the casino to see what Monte Carlo had to offer, whilst Frankie found a seat at one of the many roulette wheels. On his return, he spotted Frankie, still eagerly watching the little metal ball whirl its way round the wheel.

"Give us a few francs, Frankie! - Francs, Frankie! Get it?"

"They're on the table!"

"What do you mean, they're on the table?" Frankie sheepishly replies,

"That's all I've got left....it's on the table!"

"All you've got left! We're here for two weeks! Where's the rest of the money?"

"I've told you, it's on the table..........I've spent up!"

"I'll bloody kill you, you stupid fool! How are we going to get by for two weeks. We've not enough money to get us back to our digs!"

"Sorry! I got carried away!"

So now, a full blown argument ensues whereby Steve calls Frankie all the names he can muster until one of the croupiers leans over and says, "Excuse me sir, do you want to continue with this bet?"

"What bet?" Frankie utters.

"Do you want it to continue to ride, sir?"

"Ride? Is it still in play?"

"In play, sir. You've won nine times unbroken sir!"

"So, my bet's still in play?"

"Certainly sir, do you want to continue?"

Steve looks at Frankie and shouts, "No thanks, we'll take the money!"

So, from being an absolute plonker, Frankie has now become a genius. Not only have they won what they had lost but it's now almost tripled in value. And, true to his character of easy come easy go, they were later taking a drink in the lounge when a waiter came to attend to their needs.

"Can I get you a drink, sir?"

"Aye, I think I'll have a bottle of wine."

"Would you like white or red?"

"I'll think we'll try a drop of 'vin rouge'!"

"Any particular sort, sir?"

And Frankie came out with the best line ever in the old Casino in Monte Carlo, "Best you've got, pal!"

I think the waiter took pity on them and only got a hundred pound bottle!

Redundancy

Several years later, Frankie was made redundant, as many more thousands were during the late Seventies and early Eighties. The winter of discontent took place during 1979 because the Labour government tried to keep wage rises to a maximum of 5%. Many Trade Unions went on strike and rubbish was famously piled high in Leicester Square. Eventually a general election took place and James Callaghan was ousted by Margaret Thatcher. A march for jobs, from the North to London, was organised by the Trades Union Congress, to draw attention to the plight of the unemployed. 500 people marched from Liverpool to London on the 1st May 1981 and were joined by thousands of supporters every day. The TUC pointed out that 6,000 people every day were losing their jobs and joining the dole queues. We had issued a single titled "We want Work" to be used by the marchers on their long walk. We thought the words were perfect for workers who wanted their basic rights to a job.

"We want work we don't want dole, we're sick of the 'Old King Cole'......................now this country's got millions out of work, so I'm off on the Big Demonstration, for I will not see my trade slowly die........unemployed we demand to know why..............etc..............

The march was getting a tremendous amount of publicity and we joined it for a couple of days, when it approached and left Manchester, with guitars in hand, singing our song! We took a few of our unemployed friends with us and talked with the strikers, who were finding life very tough. So tough that they felt the march necessary to show the depth of their feelings to the country as a whole. Their antics were not getting much sympathy from Mrs. Thatcher and her government. When asked if she would meet the marchers on their arrival in London Mrs. Thatcher replied, "No!", kind of what you'd expect from her at the time. She was not known as the "Iron Lady" for nothing.

The world was in turmoil during the early years of the 1980's. Just before the march for jobs, President Reagan and three of his aides were shot outside a Washington hotel. Although close to death, he became the first serving U.S. President to survive an assassination attempt.

On the fifth day of the march, Bobby Sands, a member of the Irish Republican Army died in the Maze Prison in Belfast. He was one of ten hunger strikers who died. They were striking for special category status; to be treated as political prisoners as opposed to criminals. During his time in prison he was elected as Member of Parliament for Fermanagh and South Tyrone. The media coverage that surrounded his death resulted in a new surge of IRA activity and an escalation of the 'troubles'.

Thirteen days after the march started, Pope John Paul II was shot outside St. Peter's Square in Rome. He was in surgery for five hours but eventually recovered to go on and become the second longest serving Pope in history. He was the first non-Italian Pope since 1523 and visited 129 countries during his tenure as Pontiff.

All these things caused the march to be relegated to the lesser pages of the national newspapers. The workers though, who were losing their jobs on a daily basis, could not forget the problems that 'Maggie', who was the central character, was causing. She had recently backed down on a promise to close 23 mines but more was to follow during the next few months! On a lighter note, Bucks Fizz win the Eurovision Song Contest with 'Making your Mind up' and Bob Champion rides 'Aldaniti' to success in the Grand National at Aintree.

One of the other horses in the same race was just going over Becher's Brook when he's hit on the head with a smoked salmon! He keeps control of his mount but is hit by a bottle of Claret and two jars of chutney. In the last furlong a tin of caviar flies past his head but he's hit full in the face with a packet of 'ginger nuts'. Once over the finishing line he rushes to the race steward to complain that he's been seriously hampered!

Wembley

To give Frankie a bit of a treat I thought I'd give him a couple of days away from home. I'd been kindly given two tickets to watch England versus Brazil at Wembley. Unfortunately, Frankie doesn't know much about football – he supports Manchester United! I knew we would both enjoy the trip, so set off with no plans whatsoever apart from the match. We didn't have accommodation but knew there would be rooms available somewhere.

We arrived on Wembley Way where we found a hotel. It was expensive but as I approached the desk I could see the receptionist eyeing me up and thinking, *"No chance! He'll never be able to afford these rates and he does look a bit scruffy!"* So I was delighted when her reply to my, "Will American Express suffice?" was the classic response to the advert of the day, "That'll do nicely sir!"

It was unusually crowded because of the football match and the fact that the FA Cup final of a few days earlier had been a draw. Manchester City had played Tottenham Hotspur and drawn one goal each with Tommy Hutchison scoring both goals! The Manchester City team were staying in the same hotel as us so it was pandemonium. The replay, of the hundredth season of FA cups, was to take place two days later and would see Spurs beating City with a goal that was voted the best ever Cup Final strike. The player to take the honour was Ricardo Villa from Argentina, one of the first foreign players to participate in the English league.

I'd recently taken charge of a bright yellow MG sports car and thought it would be nice to drive down to London to 'pose' a bit. We arrived at Wembley to find the tickets were the best in the house; just behind the 'Royal Box' and we were utterly amazed to see that in the seats immediately in front of us sat several celebrities, Jimmy Tarbuck, Bernie Winters, German golfer Bernard Langer, whilst in the middle of them was the legendary Bobby Moore, captain of England's World Cup winning team of 1966. The football almost took second place to the antics of these really famous people. Eventually, Frankie built up enough courage to ask Bobby Moore for his autograph. "No problem mate! Have you got a pen?"

"Sorry pal", come Frankie's reply, "I haven't!"

"Not to worry, son, maybe next time!"

Next time! There's not going to be a next time! And so we never got the autograph of one of England's greatest footballers – don't worry, I did get the autograph of the greatest ever - Nat Lofthouse!

The match was quite a good one and England narrowly lost 1-0. My man of the match was Arsenal defender, Kenny Sansom.

The bloke is sitting in an extremely good seat for the final of the World Cup. Next to him is an empty seat. A bloke walks over to him and says, "Is that seat vacant. I'm sitting behind a huge bloke and I can't see what's happening."

"Come and join me replies the bloke, the seat belongs to my wife but she'll not be here."

"Oh, that's pity", says the bloke, "Anything the matter?"

"Well yes!" he says, "She died last week!"

"Oh, I am sorry. Could you not get a relative or friend to take her place?"

"Unfortunately not, they're all at the funeral!"

EMI

One day, Brian rang to say he was on his way to London the following day. He had some business to attend to but whilst there he was going to pop into a few recording companies to see if there was a chance of a record deal.

"Have we a cat in hell's chance of a deal?" I ask.

"Absolutely, I know quite a few of the bosses and there's a possibility that one or two of them might be interested. If I can get a couple to pay attention, then we might be able to play one against the other and get an advance against the royalties."

"Well good luck! See you in a couple of days."

And that was the last I thought about it until several days later Brian rang to say that we'd got a three year deal with EMI.

"What?" "Three years! I'm over the moon for you!"

"So what does that mean?" "It means that for the next three years you can only make records for EMI, probably the biggest recording company in the world!"

Electric and Musical Industries was in fact the fourth largest music company in the world. It got its name following a merger of "His Master's Voice", "The Gramophone Company" and "Columbia Graphaphone Company" (not to be confused with Columbia Records from America.) During the Second World War they made radar equipment, guided missiles and then latterly they made broadcasting equipment including the first ever television transmitter for the BBC.

The recording side of the business opened the doors of the world famous Abbey Road studios in 1931 and have been responsible for some of the greatest recordings of all time, including Sir Edward Elgar, The London Symphony

Orchestra, Cliff Richards and the Beatles..........and then we turned up!

Bob Barratt, our Producer, had spent some time in our area to see what we could do and to decide on a list of songs that we could record. He was a very polite and respectful gentleman who found our act to be quite entertaining. He would meet us at a gig and chat about content, then disappear to his hotel and we wouldn't see him until our next gig a few days later. Bob had spent the intervening couple of days pursuing his favourite hobby........buses!

When asked he would enthuse, "Oh, I got up this morning and caught the number 37 to Liverpool. I then got on the 313 from there to Southport and spent the rest of the day on the 434 from Southport back to Warrington!"

"Why?"

"Oh, it's wonderful! The 37 was a 'Lancashire United Transport' double decker! The LUT livery is an orangey red colour whilst the 'Ribble' buses round this area will have a purple livery with a beige hoop around their girth. I don't know if you know but horse drawn buses, not trams, were active in the early 1800's followed by steam and electric trolleybuses!"

"How fascinating!"

"Yes, the buses we know today originated at the beginning of the twentieth century and haven't changed much since then. They got their name from the Latin "Omnibus" which is also very interesting in its' own way."

"Oh!"

"Yes, one of the first Bus stations in France was in Nantes. The station stood just outside a Hatters shop named "Omnes Omnibus", two Latin words meaning "all" and "for all". Locals soon gave the name to the vehicles that stopped regularly outside the premises and the name stuck!"

"Well that's absolutely wonderful! Will you just excuse me; I need to go to the toilet!"

We were to spend many exhilarating sessions talking about buses unless I fell asleep which was quite regularly! I'd heard of train and plane spotters but never buses! Everyone to their own as they say!

He might have been a bit of a nerd when it came to buses but in the recording studio Bob came to the fore. He knew every switch and every slider in the famous Abbey Road Studio number One. This was a huge room that could be divided into smaller booths, by great moveable screens, so that the sound from one performer would not impinge on the sound of another. From the tiny box of a studio in Mid Wales to this cathedral of a studio in London, we had moved quite a way in a very short space of time.

At the television studios we had extra musicians and so too here! They mustn't have thought we were capable on our own! A pianist, drummer and a couple of guitarists augmented what we did so as to add to the fullness of the sound. During conversation with them we were to realise that they were some of the best musicians in the capital and spent most of their lives within the hallowed halls of Abbey Road. They'd recorded with all the great names of the British music scene and would mention their names but not with arrogance. They were just the same as the ones in Manchester.

"The best musicians in the world are here in London and there are lots of them," said Bob, "so why employ someone who's not pleasant!"

Always with a brand new, or not so brand new joke at hand, whenever necessary, these musicians worked together a lot of the time and were all mates.

"Did you hear the one about the 'muso' who went on holiday to the Caribbean?", says the guitarist. "He gets off the plane and all he can hear is drums. He goes to the beach – drums! After his evening meal the drums are still playing. All through the night – drums. He finally goes to reception and complains, "What's with the drums! Do they ever stop? They're driving me mad!"

The receptionist counters, "No the drums must never stop, drums are good! Very bad if drums stop!"

"Why?" asks the bloke.

"Because when drums stop, bass solo begins!"

"Funny!" says the bass player, "How can you tell when a drummer's at the door?"

"Don't know!"

"The knocking speeds up!"

Light hearted banter that makes a day more enjoyable, most of the time.

"That Tony sings a bit like Eric Morecambe!"

"What do you mean?"

"Well, he sings all the right notes but not necessarily in the right order!"

This continues for most of the day when there are quiet periods. Otherwise they are totally conscientious and professional in their attitude to work.

1982

Margaret Thatcher had defeated big Jim Callaghan, the tallest British Prime minister, in the election of 1979 and for almost twenty years she ruled Britain with an iron fist. Many were against her harsh policies and the first few years of her tenure saw her popularity wane due to recession and high unemployment. However, a small economic recovery and an incident that took place many thousands of miles away would see the 'Iron Lady's' popularity soar.

On the 2nd April 1982, Argentine forces invaded the Falkland Islands, South Georgia and the South Sandwich islands leading to the 'Falklands War'. 'Maggie' decided that, rather than give up this tiny group of islands in the South Atlantic, we would put together a 'task force' to re-take what belonged to us. The conflict lasted 74 days and ended with the Argentine surrender on 14th June 1982, which returned the islands back to British control at the cost of 649 Argentinian military, 255 British service personnel and three Falkland islanders.

From that point onwards Thatcher's popularity soared and she decided to take the unions 'head on' and the miners were to be the victims of her wrath. Thatcher had appointed Ian McGregor, a Scottish-American, as head of the National Coal Board. He had previously headed British Steel and had halved the workforce. The leader of the National Union of Miners, Arthur Scargill, who had a better haircut than Bobby Charlton, felt that this would happen to the miners and so decided to strike (without a ballot), for more money. The strike opened up deep divisions within British society and caused terrible bitterness in many areas of the country. Eventually, Thatcher broke the miners and, in turn, weakened the power of the Trade Unions in this country forever.

She was one of the most dominant figure in 20th century British politics, serving three terms as leader. She advocated privatisation of state owned businesses and reduction of taxes. These measures reduced inflation but dramatically increased unemployment during her period in power. She narrowly escaped death in 1984 when an IRA bomb exploded in the hotel she was staying in during the Conservative party annual conference. Towards the end of her term as leader, her policies, especially the dreaded 'Poll Tax', led to a revolt amongst the party which eventually led to a leadership challenge and her resignation. She was succeeded by John Major. Here are some of her very famous quotes:

"Being powerful is like being a lady. If you have to tell people you are, you aren't!"

"I owe nothing to Women's Lib!"

"It may be the cock that crows, but it is the hen that lays the eggs!"

"I'm extraordinarily patient, provided I get my own way in the end!"

And finally:

"If you want something said, ask a man; if you want something done, ask a woman!"

Takamine

That's pronounced "taka meeny" and it's the name of a Japanese made guitar. They started in the 1970's and eventually broke into the British market. A local Bolton firm secured distribution rights throughout the UK and, to publicise the instruments, gave several away to well known artists. We were, by this time, very popular and so the company rang us and offered us 6 guitars, free of course, so that we would use the instruments on stage.

We agreed, and to make it official, the top executive of Takamine came over from Japan to present the guitars. He thought it would be nice to have a meal together and get to know the recipients of their skilled workforce. Our manager at the time decided that we should meet at a top Manchester restaurant and that was arranged.

When the day arrived, there were several people from the Japanese makers including Mr. Mass Hirade, the company president and representatives from the Bolton distributors. The four members of our group and our manager made the total number of diners around the twenty mark. We met in the foyer of the Piccadilly hotel and formal introductions were made. Mr. Hirade spoke very basic English but could get by. There were a lot of smiles and even more bowing before we took our places around a huge dining table. I was sitting next to our manager, Brian, who in turn sat opposite Mass and pleasantries were exchanged. Brian was attired in his best beige suit with waistcoat, the height of fashion at the time. During the main course, which was the tenderest fillet steak that I had ever tasted, I spotted Brian cutting through his piece of meat. All of a sudden the knife slipped on the plate and a huge piece of fillet shot off the table. Everyone was concerned that Brian hadn't cut himself but he was more anxious that the meat hadn't stained his new suit! Mr. Hirade thought it was quite amusing and nodded several times before leaning over to his sidekick and spouting out in Japanese. He was probably saying that he was dealing with a bunch of stupid English nutters!

The rest of the afternoon went without incident and everyone laughed and joked until late in the afternoon. Eventually, Mr. Hirade decided to put an end to the proceedings. He stood up, thanked us for our hospitality and for accepting his guitars. Our manager, Brian, stood up to reciprocate his thanks and hoped that we would meet again soon. Wishing us all luck for the future, Brian leaned across the table took Mass by the hand and as he shook his hand a huge piece of fillet steak slipped out of his jacket sleeve and fell into Mr. Hirade's coffee!

He gave a startled look around the table, smiled, bowed several times and got out of the building as fast as he could! We never saw him again!

The Takamine company was founded in 1962 at the base of Mount Takamine in Sakashita, Japan. By 1978 they were one of the first companies to introduce acoustic-electric models as they pioneered the design of a pre-amp equaliser component. Basically, it means you can play it plugged in and it will be electrified but it can also be played acoustically. Mr. Mass Hirade joined the company in 1968 and set up an overseas division several years later, doing business directly with distributors before becoming President of the company in 1978. I don't think he ever came to Westhoughton again!

74

Holiday

Frankie and I had decided to take a holiday to the South of France. We were going to drive all the way via the ferry from Dover. After several perusals of the map of Europe, we decided it might be better if we sailed from Plymouth to Santander in Northern Spain. Looking at the map, it seemed much nearer to go via Northern Spain. Two friends decided to accompany us, so we were travelling in two cars, my MG and Phil's Jaguar. Phil, who we all called 'Sandbagger' would be travelling in his car with 'Boothy' otherwise known as Ray. His Jaguar wasn't superstar material but a clapped out version that drank petrol and broke down frequently!

We made our way from Westhoughton to Portsmouth without much trouble and settled down to a very long ferry journey which lasted 24 hours. We only had a reclining chair to rest in, so by the time we reached Spain we were all shattered. Out through customs and along the fabulous motorways of Northern Spain, over the Pyrenees and not too long a trip down the coast of Southern France to a place called Sainte Maxime. This is a small town on the Gulf of Saint Tropez that was founded around 1000 A.D. by monks, who built a monastery and named the place after one of their saints, Maxime. Its beach was the centre of 'Operation Dragoon' during the Second World War, which was mounted to liberate Southern France. There are memorials all along the beaches to honour those liberating US troops.

But we weren't there to sight see, we were there to lounge on the beaches during the day and frequent the bars at night! Early in the trip we came upon a ram-shackled wooden hut adjoining the beach, owned by an elderly French bloke who sat gloomily at the bar. We'd been there about half an hour when the bloke, in very broken English, said he was closing for the night. Frankie approached the gentleman and said that we'd only just arrived and was there any chance of staying open for another hour.

"Another hour, I want to go home to my wife!"

"But we are spending money with you, and we are very good customers. We will come back every night if you stay open for a while!"

"Just for a few more minutes then I must go home. I am very tired!"

So we get a couple of rounds in and we can see Jean Luc; we'd got his name by this time, keep looking at his watch.

Eventually he strolls over to our table, "I must go home now. I will leave the keys for you to lock up. Please drop them through the door when you leave. If you want more beer please leave the money by the till!"

And off he strolls leaving us all dumbfounded.

"Right!" calls Frankie, "I'm in charge! If you want a drink you pay for it. If you've not got the right change then you must forfeit it and pay more. Jean Luc has been great with us so we must not abuse his trust."

So, for the rest of the evening we drink and drink. A few new customers arrive and Frankie takes charge behind the bar with the same rules. Pay the right money or pay more but you'll not get a drink otherwise. Rules sorted! So we have a fabulous night with lots of beer drunk and no trouble whatsoever. Eventually it's time to retire to our tent. Oh, I forgot to tell you, we were camping! So we wash all the glasses, tidy all the tables and chairs and leave a pile of francs next to the till (still francs, not euros yet!)

We've hired a large tent for the four of us at a campsite just up the road. We get back and collapse into our sleeping bags! Unfortunately, at eight o'clock in the morning, it is like an oven in the tent and although we'd like to stay there till tea time we have to get up. We stagger to the beach and find some very comfortable loungers which weren't too expensive to hire and settle down back to sleep. By evening time we all looked like lobsters! We hadn't got round to putting the sun tan oil on and we were all in considerable pain.

We are making our way back to the campsite for a change of clothes when we hear a shout, "Frankie! Frankie!"

"What's that?" says Boothy, "It sounds like somebody wants Keith!"

"Frankie! Frankie!" It's Jean Luc chasing us down the beach. "Oh, my God, has he been broken into. Did we leave the keys? Has somebody stolen the money?" Jean Luc catches us up and hugs Frankie, "My friend! That was the best night's takings I have ever had! The place was clean and the glasses were washed! Please come back anytime – the place is yours – you can have a set of keys to keep – and tonight the first two rounds are on me!"

So that was the night times sorted out. Keith had made a friend and we had somewhere to go at night! Nothing else of great importance happened for the next two weeks apart from the bloke that said that large beef tomatoes were the perfect cure for sunburn. We'd cut one of these tomatoes in half and rub them all over our skin which did nothing to relieve the burning but covered our bodies in small tomato pips!

On our return to Blighty, Boothy and Sandbagger decided they were going to take home lots of duty free. I explained to Frankie that I was only willing to take our limit through customs, no more no less!

"Fine by me!" says Frankie, "All I need is a packet of cigs for my dad and a bottle of brandy for my mam."

So we carefully filled our boot with the maximum allowance but no more. On the other hand, Ray and Phil piled as much contraband in their car as they could. Many hundreds of cigarettes and tobacco, bottles of whiskey, rum brandy, you name it, they had it!

We eventually arrive at Portsmouth and we can see that the militia are out in force! There are police, customs officers and officials of every sort. We begin to queue in our lane and Sandbagger pushes and pushes his way through the traffic to get directly behind me in line. I'm not looking to get through this lot easily!

"You, sir! Yellow MG, into this lane please!"

I leave the main queue and go where he tells me, with Sandbagger in close pursuit! I find myself in a sort of garage affair with an inspection pit below and am asked to drive over the trench. Out from every orifice appears inspectors who begin to search my vehicle with a fine tooth comb. They've got mirrors to look behind wheel arches, screwdrivers to take off facia boards and dashboards. They empty everything from the boot and go through the baggage item by item. They lift up carpets and search under the spare wheel. In fact, they leave absolutely nothing untouched! It takes almost an hour but as the time goes by, I'm feeling more nervous for the car behind than for me!

Eventually, they release me from their custody and send me on my way with a "Good morning, sir, sorry for the inconvenience, pleasant journey!"

We drive just up the road, trying not to look too conspicuous, when Sandbagger pulls up alongside me!

"What happened to you, you lucky beggar. How did you get here so fast?"

"Well, the bloke asked me where I was going and when I said that I was with you he just said, 'off you go! Have a nice day!'"

Pantomime

Bookings are coming thick and fast and we don't have a minute to spare. Then we get a phone call from Brian, our manager, "Do you fancy doing panto?"

"Pantomime? Where?"

"Blackpool Grand want you. It should be good; six weeks work with two shows a day!"

"But we've never done panto, how will we cope?"

"Same as everyone else; just a bit of acting and dancing, it'll be a doddle! It's behind you!"

"Oh, no it isn't!"

"Oh, yes it is!" A bit of acting and dancing?? Never done anything like that before but I'll have a go at anything!

So that was our introduction to pantomime! We were to be top of the bill at the recently opened and refurbished Grand theatre in Blackpool. There had been a long running argument between developers and the "friends" of the theatre to either keep the theatre as it was originally intended or replace it with a multi-storey car park. Fortunately the friends were successful and following refurbishment, the Grade 2 listed building opened as a Bingo Hall and then as the theatre you see today. It was built in 1893/4 at a cost of £20,000 by Frank Matcham, who was to be the designer of some of Britain's most beautiful emporiums including The London Palladium, Buxton's Opera House, the Gaiety Theatre on the Isle of Man and the Hackney Empire to name but a few. Matcham had been challenged by the owner, Mr. Thomas Sergenson to build the "prettiest theatre in the land". He used a new 'cantilever' design technology which meant that the auditorium could be built without the use of pillars that restricted an audience's view.

The theatre was a very successful venture until after the Second World War, when the advent of television saw its demise. Plans were drawn up to demolish the building until the "friends" got together to save this magnificent theatre which is today known as the National Theatre of Variety.

So we arrive two weeks before the panto season for rehearsals. This tended to be a fairly haphazard affair. The 'regulars' just went about their business as usual, preparing costumes, make-up, props etc. whilst we newcomers sat around twiddling our thumbs. We did some script practice but that tended to change on a daily basis. Everyone fought for the best lines whilst we sat back and watched the "luvvies" argue! As a group of singers we saw ourselves as a "turn" meaning an act that performs songs. "Luvvies" on the other hand were actors and felt far superior to us mere mortals. We found it quite amusing but we were being left behind when it came to the performance. The greatest problem was to get us to dance! I wasn't too bad but Denis and David hated it and had great difficulty keeping step. The only time we felt comfortable was when we were singing as a group but during the show that was only intermittently.

Eventually we began to get the hang of it and felt that we were becoming more accomplished. The season was going well with box office records being broken for ticket sales. Even though we were enjoying our time at this beautiful theatre I always felt that this was not what we formed a group for, although it did have its lighter moments.

The particular pantomime was "Cinderella" featuring the magical costume changes when "Cinders" is allowed to go to the ball. The coaches were being pulled by two beautiful Shetland ponies that were housed in a trailer outside the stage door. When it came to the end of the first half they were brought onto side stage and guided on for the finale which regularly ended with one of them emptying their bowels on stage which generally brought a roar of approval from the crowd.

During one scene, Cinderella is talking to Buttons, who was being played by Norman. They were alone on stage and, sinking down to the floor in an embrace, Norman sings "When you wish upon a Star." The auditorium is blacked out and the pair have a solitary spot light to pinpoint them; a very poignant part in the whole show. One particular night Norman is half way through his rendition when a rather large lady on the front row breaks wind! Unfortunately it was very loud and most of the packed audience heard the blast, bringing pandemonium as they break into uncontrollable laughter. Both Buttons and Cinders, together with the entire orchestra in the pit, were falling about in side splitting chaos, whilst the lady in question is looking around in wonderment as to what was going on. Eventually everyone composes themselves and Norman continues .... "Like a bolt out of the blue!" reducing everyone to tears again!

During another 'panto' season in Ashton-under-Lyne, we were joined on stage by "Old Mother Riley" played by Roy Rolland. Roy was understudy to the original Old Mother Riley, Arthur Lucan. Old Mother Riley was an Irish washerwoman who had very eccentric ways, facial and bodily contortions and malapropism filled tirades against all who displeased her. The original act was a double headed affair with Lucan's wife, Kitty McShane, playing Old Mother Riley's daughter. There were times when he was so drunk that Roy would take to the stage in his place and no-one, including Kitty could tell the difference. The problem was, Kitty had hated him for many years and promised to shoot him on stage, with a loaded pistol she kept in her handbag. There were times, therefore, when Roy actually feared for his life! This team finally split through Kitty's infidelity and Lucan's drinking habits. He eventually dropped dead in the wings of the Tivoli theatre in Hull on 17th May 1954. Roy Rolland had played understudy to Lucan for many years and was his double in films. The final film was "Mother Riley meets the Vampire" starring Bela Lugosi and was shot in 1952. Following Lucan's death, Rolland took over as the washerwoman with continued success. For a summer season Danny la Rue recreated the role of Kitty McShane in Blackpool. Roy Rolland continued the success of the character in Yorkshire television's Junior Showtime during the 1970s.

We had agreed to do pantomime with Old Mother Riley, as the dame, of course and we were all looking forward to working with such a star of music hall. Unfortunately, with only two days to go before the opening night, Roy rang in to say he was ill and would not be able to do the show. Panic ensued and we ended rehearsals with absolutely no idea who would fill in the gaping holes in the script that his character would fill. Our Producer, Brian, left saying that he would sort something out by tomorrow. It would be extremely tight but he was convinced he could find the perfect substitute.

The following morning we were due to do a dress rehearsal so we gathered on stage to discuss last minute hitches with the stage crew. As we all congregated on stage a little old man, in a crombie overcoat, wearing a trilby at a rakish angle and carrying a supermarket plastic bag, hobbled down the central aisle. At first we thought someone had walked in from the streets when our producer said, "Ladies and gentlemen, please welcome our new dame, Alex Munro!"

Passing over a script to Alex he boomed "Act One beginners!"

And so began the worst rehearsal I'd ever been involved in! Alex couldn't see his script because he'd left his glasses on the bus! He couldn't remember any lines and looked completely lost. He'd discarded his overcoat to reveal a long sleeved cardigan with holes in both elbows. On occasions he was seen approaching his plastic bag and taking a quiet swig from its contents. All the time he continued saying, "Don't worry about me boys, just feed me a line and I'll be alright!" So we'd feed him a line and he would look around the stage to see who's turn it was!

"This is not going to work!" I plead with the producer, "Can we not just cut out his scenes and we'll fill in with a few songs?"

"He just needs a few days to learn the script", came the reply.

"But the show opens tomorrow night!"

"I think he'll be alright when he's got an audience!"

"There'll not be an audience for long if he's as bad as that!" I retort.

"Just give him a bit of time" implores Brian.

"That's the one thing we've not got", I plead.

"He might have been a star once but he's an old bloke who can hardly walk never mind run around the stage!"

But the producer is adamant and the rehearsal continues to go downhill for the rest of the day. Eventually we decide to go home and Alex shouts to us as we leave the theatre, "Don't worry boys, just feed me a line and then leave it all to me!"

God help us all! It's going to be a disaster. The newspaper reporters are coming tomorrow night and they are going to slate us!

So we plod through the next day as we had left the previous evening, with Alex seemingly unable to do anything right. We approach the evening performance and first night nerves kick in with almost everybody. We were more concerned about the press. They would give us a spanking tonight and we couldn't use the illness of Roy Rolland to escape our punishment.

"Don't worry boys! Just feed me a line and leave it all to me" reiterates Alex.

The opening music plays as a sell out audience takes to their seats. The curtains open and the show begins. Adrenaline takes over and we decide to make the show a success without the aid of Alex. We'll just keep talking and cover up any mistakes he's bound to make.

So the Houghton Weavers take to the stage to rapturous applause and we go through the opening scenes with a flourish. As we approach the end of our short opening routine we sing a song and shout for Old Mother Riley.

Alex Munro bounces onto stage and completely captivates the audience from the second he appears. He is in complete control of all around him. The metamorphosis from hobbling pensioner to enthralling 'Dame' is complete! For the rest of the night he completely takes over the stage. Occasionally he allows us a few lines of dialogue and waits for a breath then he's back to his superb best. I don't think I could ever judge anyone from first impressions ever again. The man was an utter genius with the audience and received a standing ovation from the crowd at the end of the night. As we walked off stage following the final curtain call, Alex, with a twinkle in the eye said, "I told you not to worry boys!"

The following morning papers gave us a few lines of praise and other members of the cast got a sporadic comment but all the praise was heaped on the incredible Alex Munro.

Alex was born in Shettleston, Glasgow in 1911 and formed an acrobatic trio with his brother, Archie and sister, June. They joined Florrie Forde's music hall company with Flanagan and Allen and toured extensively. During World War 2 he toured with the RAF show "Contact" and had his own Radio series titled 'The Size of It'. Eventually Alex made his home in Llandudno and he had a very successful show which ran for 30 years.

And we were worried that he couldn't hack it!

The pantomime was going very well with extremely good 'houses' due to the write ups in the local papers. Then we got the news that Roy Rolland had recovered from his illness and was due to return the following day.

"So what's going to happen to Alex?"

"I'm afraid he's going to have to go!"

"But you can't sack him! Everybody loves him and he's the star of the show!"

"Unfortunately we have a contract with Roy, so Alex must go!"

"So who's going to tell him?"

"I'm afraid that task has fallen to me," replied Brian. We break for coffee and as we walk onto stage to leave the theatre by the front door, Alex walks across the auditorium with overcoat, trilby and plastic bag in hand.

"Morning boys, I'm just off!"

"Off where?" I enquire.

"Back to Llandudno! I've just been given the last card in the pack!"

He raised his trilby and walked through the door without a backward glance.

We never saw him again.

So from that day, to the end of the season, Roy Rolland returned to take his place as Dame. Just like Alex and a lot of the old stagers he was incredible. We were all in awe of these professional actor/comedians who had worked in every situation throughout their acting careers. Their apprenticeships had lasted 30, 40 or even 50 years and there was so much to be learned from these true gems of theatre-land.

On one night during this particular run, there was a power cut. They were fairly commonplace during the late 70s and early 80s. Most power cuts in a domestic situation were awkward but no great discomfort other than one couldn't have a bath when needed, unless you had a coal fire with a back boiler! In a theatre, it was a different situation. All the lights went out and the show had to stop! Or did it? The management were panicking with the thought that they would have to reimburse everyone in the crowd. Although there was only around fifteen or twenty minutes left of the show a full refund was a distinct possibility. We walked onto stage to calm the audience and asked if all the usherettes would come to the front of the stage. They proceeded to shine their torches on us for the final twenty minutes and we performed some of our favourites which were received with enthusiasm. Some of the old stagers we'd worked with had taught us to be prepared for any situation and that, 'the show must go on!'

Robin Hood

During this same pantomime I was cast as Robin Hood. I wore green tights and thigh length boots together with green tunic and feathered cap. During the show I was engaged in a stage fight with the Sherriff of Nottingham, a dastardly actor named Hugo Myatt. The sword fight had been rehearsed for many, many hours as it was quite dangerous. Both Hugo and I used heavy metal swords so that it would be reasonably authentic. Although the swords were extremely blunt they were rather weighty and had a pointed end.

We had a routine that went something like, to the right - up strike, down strike, up to the left, strike, down strike, etc. Following several blows, the sheriff forces me to the ground and asks me to surrender to which I refuse. He takes me prisoner and that's more or less it – don't worry! I win in the end!

On one particular night, as I'm falling to the floor, I slip and bang my elbow on the stage. This causes my sword to fly out of my grasp and into the crowd! It only misses the musical director in the pit because he ducks to one side. The weapon continues to fly towards the audience. Everything now goes into slow motion.

I can see the blade piercing an old lady on the front row and embedding her in her seat. Newspapers will report that Robin Hood has murdered a member of the audience. I'll be thrown in jail like a common criminal. Maid Marian would probably end up marrying the Sheriff and Old Mother Riley will never speak to me again!

The blade continues to fly out and lands harmlessly in the aisle!

It's very dangerous being an actor!

It's like the actor who rings his girlfriend's father to ask for her hand in marriage.

"I'd never let my daughter marry an actor", retorts the father.

"Maybe if you saw me perform you might change your mind, sir?"

So the guy goes to the theatre the same night and rings back the following morning.

"I've changed my mind son, you can have my daughter's hand in marriage."

"Why the change of mind?" asks the lad.

"Because, after last nights' performance I've realised that you're not an actor!"

Southport Theatre

The Southport theatre was built in 1973 as an addition to the Floral Hall that originated in the 1930's. There has been a major investment of £40million recently, which has seen major renovations and the building of a hotel complex on the site. We were asked to do a show in the theatre which we duly obliged. Some years later we embarked on a summer season in the Floral Hall that ran for many years.

On our original visit to the theatre we were in conversation with the staff. They told of the opening night a couple of years before. A host of celebrities had been booked and they arrived during the day for dress rehearsals with the orchestra. They would run through their music and amend any lingering problems. Then it was into the dressing room to prepare for the evening performance. The only problem was that there were no changing rooms. Although the theatre had won several design awards from the European Commission, when the artistes went backstage, following their run through, they were confronted with a brick wall! They had forgotten to build dressing rooms, so for the next few years all participants of the theatre had to change in a 'porta-cabin' attached to a hole in the back wall!

Around that time, we were on stage at this same theatre, when Norman asked if there was anyone in the auditorium from Wigan. Quite a few hands were seen in the crowd. Norman continued, "Well I'd like to congratulate Wigan Athletic on gaining election to the football league."

I pulled him to one side and reminded him, "Don't you realise it was Southport who were relegated, you fool!"

The audience were with us all the way – we finally shook them off at the station!

Wigan Athletic was formed in 1932 following the demise of Wigan Borough. They bought their ground and played for many years at Springfield Park. Their first honours were gained in 1933/4 when they won the Cheshire league. In 1968 they were founder members of the Northern Premier League and won the title in 1970/1. Prior to automatic promotion in 1987 any team from the lower leagues had to apply for inclusion. Following 34 failed attempts they actually applied for election to the Scottish Second Division. Although they failed to gain election they did gain a lot of publicity. I think the real reason was that nobody from north of the border could understand them!

Eventually they gained admission to the football league on 2nd June 1978, at the expense of Southport. In February 1995, local millionaire and businessman, Dave Whelan, purchased the club and grandly announced that his aim was Premiership football. He was widely ridiculed but he was the one who had the last laugh. With the help of three Spanish players, including Roberto Martinez, who were nicknamed the three Amigos, they eventually made it to the promised land of the Premiership in 2005.

Junior Football

This reminds me of the time I was a youngster. We organised a football league in Westhoughton. There were four teams! All were connected to local churches. I played for the Sacred Heart which was the Catholic team, whilst the Church of England had two representatives in St. Bartholomew's and St. Thomas's. The team making up the quartet were the Trinity Wesleyan church. We played each other every couple of weeks and amassed goal tallies you would not believe. Scores of 22-23 were not uncommon! It was great fun and the organisers amongst us were very professional in their attitude towards the games. Pitches were inspected as to their suitability, all strips were procured so that there would be no clashes in shirt colour and finally, referees, usually parents, were paid a few pence for officiating at the eagerly fought contests.

Each team had a representative who attended meetings (usually in the field behind the park). On one occasion there was a knockout competition with a cup final. We all reached the semi's which was a major feat; on second thoughts not that major as there were only four teams in the competition! Sacred Heart, with team captain Gerald fought through to the final against St. Bartholomew's, who were captained by a friend, Paul Gaskell. Well they were all friends! We sometimes shared the oranges at half time!

My brother, James and his mate Gerald, built a dug-out for the team manager on the half way line for the occasion and invited the local Parish Priest to attend, to judge the 'man of the match'. Father O'Leary kindly agreed to join us on the morning of the match and sheltered in the newly built dug-out. Mr. Ivers was the referee for the game. He was a lovely man but unfortunately, profoundly deaf, which didn't help when arguments ensued. The whistle went and everyone ran around like headless chickens for an hour and a half! By the end of the game tensions were at an incredible high as the teams were tied 21-21. Extra time was looming when the referee awarded a penalty to Sacred Heart and, at the same time, blew the whistle for the end of the match.

If you know the rules of the game, which I'm sure, quite a few of you do, then you'll know that the kick of the ball will be the last play in the game. In other words, if the ball goes straight in the net, it's a goal, if it doesn't, that's the end of proceedings. So Taffy, our expert penalty taker, marches up to take the penalty. Jack Ensor, who was to become one of the best goalkeepers in Westhoughton, faced him. Mr. Ivers blows the whistle, Taffy runs up and smacks the ball goalwards. Jack flies to his right and parries the shot; Ian runs in and puts the rebound into the back of the net!

Mr. Ivers blows the whistle and confirms that the goal stands.

"But you can't do that, it's not a goal. You blew the whistle to end the match!"

"He's given the goal so Sacred Heart has won!"

"But ref, it's not a goal!"

"He can't hear you!"

"What?"

"He can't hear you!"

"Who can't hear me?"

"The ref!"

So the Sacred Heart players run joyfully towards Father O'Leary to collect their trophy whilst the St. Bartholomew's players scream at the ref to play extra time.

"Congratulations boys. Hope to see you all at mass on Sunday?"

"Yes father, thank you father!"

"Never mind mass on Sunday, we demand to speak to the league organiser!"

"Well he's over there. The one holding the cup in the air!"

Well, it's only a game!

There was a footballer walking down the street when he comes across a blazing house. From the upstairs window a voice screams, "Help me! Help me save my baby!"

"Don't worry", shouts the footballer, "I'm a professional goalkeeper. Throw the baby to me and I'll catch it!"

"Are you sure?" cries the woman.

"No problem! I've never dropped a ball in my life!"

So the woman gently tosses her child down to the waiting bloke below, who catches it easily, smiles up at the woman, bounces the bundle three times and kicks it thirty yards down the street!

Isle of Man

Many years later, that losing captain had never forgiven me for
their loss in that pulsating match but we were still friends. Paul
now lived on the Isle of Man and worked for the local Manx
newspaper. He had worked for the paper in Bolton but got a
job with the Manx newspaper. Funnily enough, when he left
Bolton, it was David from the Weavers group who got his job.
After a few years, Paul went to work for the casino on the
island as their head of entertainment. Not forgetting our
friendship, he invited us over as part of their summer season of
entertainment.

So we were going to the Isle of Man for the very first time!

We are going via the ferry from Liverpool which will be
very exciting. We arrive at the Pier Head well in advance of
the departure time. The dock is actually a 'floating dock' as the
tides come in and out of the River Mersey. The thing is
bobbing about quite severely and it looks like we are in for a
bouncy trip! So the boat's bobbing up and down and the dock
is bobbing up and down. Unfortunately, they weren't bobbing
up and down at the same time! We, or should I say Phil, has to
negotiate driving down, or up as the case may be at the time,
along a fairly flimsy piece of planking to hit the deck of the
boat when they are both reasonably adjacent!

It took quite a while to line up but he eventually got us up
the ramp and into the hold. We line up our vehicle, lock it up
and proceed to the lounge which was up about three flights of
steps. If you remember going in the 'Fun House' at Blackpool
or Southport Pleasure Beach, then you will have experienced
the journey up those steps. You take one step up but the

motion of the vessel is downward so it becomes quite an achievement getting from bottom to top!

We eventually arrive in quite a large, circular lounge at the front of the ship, or prow if you want the nautical version! There's a continual sofa that goes around the perimeter of the room with adjacent tables and chairs that are bolted down to the floor. The rest of the area is covered by tables and chairs that are all fastened to the deck. At the front of the area is a small hatch in the centre serving teas and snacks. On either side of this small aperture are steps leading up to the deck. We know that things are going to be bad when a waiter leans into the hatch and takes a pile of brown paper bags from his assistant. He then proceeds to put several of these bags on each table in the room!

"What's he doing?"

"What do you think?"

"Well, has he put those bags out to collect the rubbish?"

"No, I don't think so, but it is to collect something!"

"What?"

"Just look around the room and you'll soon work it out!"

So our vessel makes its way to the Irish Sea via the Mersey estuary. As we approach the main body of water, our vessel seems to take a mind of its own. It begins to move in places where I don't think it was designed to go, heaving, rolling, tossing and turning. Very slowly the room begins to look deserted as the passengers decide to find a space of their own where they can shout for 'Hughie'. The colour of the faces of those that are afraid to move, slowly changes from the normal pinkish to the grey associated with Dracula and eventually the Incredible Hulk's green hue!

Philip and I are quite happy with the movement of the ship and we are becoming more and more amused with the antics of the passengers and other members of the group.

"Help me!" cries Norman, "What can I do?"

"I've heard that the best position is on your back, so why don't you go out on deck and lie down!"

"Preferably at the back, or the stern, as Long John Silver would say!"

"Why the back?"

"Because that's where the engines are and the weight will keep everything steadier down there! Oh and by the way, it's Long John Saliva! If not it's his spitting image!"

"I really needed that one, thanks!"

"Don't worry; it won't take long, only about four hours!"

The Irish Sea is of great importance in many ways. Over 12 million passengers and 17 million tonnes of freight sail over it every year. It is used for power generation in the form of wind farms and nuclear plants. It is incredibly rich in wildlife such as mussels, scallops, shrimps and cockles, whilst the adjoining estuaries are important nurseries for sea bass, herring and flatfish. Whales, dolphins, porpoises and basking sharks frequent the area because of the profusion of plankton that drift into the sea. There is an immense diversity of crabs, cuttlefish and other invertebrates whilst several species of seal live in and around its shores. There are at least twenty-one species of seabird that regularly nest on the cliffs and beaches. With this multitude of nature abounding it is quite sad to report that 'Greenpeace' have described it as the most contaminated sea in the world. Mostly from Sellafield, the low level radioactive waste is being reduced considerably year on year.

It is argued that the risks are minimal and that heavy consumption of locally sourced seafood generates a 1 in 18 million chance of causing cancer. Apparently, the general risk of contracting cancer in Ireland is 1 in 522, so it seems to me that you're better off eating loads of seafood – it's better than taking vitamins!

Going back to our seasick passengers.......I quickly get sidetracked!......On arrival in Douglas both Norman and Denis insisted that they would never sail again!

"If I can't fly home, I'm going to stay here till the day I die!" was Denis's heartfelt plea!

He did fly home and came back several times.......but only ever by plane!

The Isle of Man was a Mecca for English tourists in the 50s and 60s, as a place where young people could holiday away from home. My sister regularly went there on holiday. As we marched into the 70s and 80s, package holidays to the Costa Brava became more of the norm and the island changed its focus from holidays to investments, becoming a hideaway for the rich. Paul loved telling me the story about the multi millionaire who visited the casino once every few months. On this particular night he arrived without money. Paul said that his credit was good and that he didn't need to worry. At the end of the evening he approached Paul with a huge pile of chips. After counting out the chips and subtracting what he owed the casino, the gentleman had won £28,000.00. Unfortunately Paul hadn't got that much cash available on the night and gave the bloke a cheque for £20,000.00 and cash to the value of £8,000.00.

Six months later, our friendly millionaire turned up one night to play the tables. Again he approached Paul and said that he'd forgotten to bring out any cash. Again Paul re-iterated that his credit was good and told him to carry on. Our rich friend thanked him and was about to walk away, when he put his hand in his pocket and pulled out the cheque for £20,000.00, It had been in his pocket for six months and he'd completely forgotten about it! I wonder how many readers could forget that they had twenty grand in their pocket! I think most of us would agree that bills travel through the post at twice the speed of cheques!

The Isle of Man lies in the middle of the Irish Sea and from the summit of its highest mountain, Snaefell, there's an old saying that you can see six and some say seven, kingdoms. I'll not let you dwell on that one but tell you that they are, Mann, Scotland, Ireland, England, Wales and looking upwards, the kingdom of Heaven. The seventh is the kingdom of Neptune or the kingdom of the sea! Legend has it that the island was formed when the Irish giant Finn MacCooil threw a chunk of Ireland towards Scotland and it fell short! The island arguably gets its name from the Celtic Sea God, Manannan Mac Lir who, to protect the island, shrouded it in a cloak of mist. Well, I've heard of some excuses for bad weather! The island is self governing and has the oldest continuous parliament in the world, the Tynwald.

Besides the capital, Douglas, you'll find Europe's most preserved medieval castle in Castle Rushen, the largest working waterwheel in the world at Laxey, Celtic crosses and Viking burial grounds, electric railways, horse drawn trams, cats with a minute tail (Stumpy) or no tail at all (Rumpy), sheep with four and sometimes six horns, the native Loaghtan sheep, loads of basking sharks in summer but still the most famous thing to come out of the island is the famous Tourist Trophy or TT races. The event takes place in late May and early June and is now an international road race event. It began in 1907 attracting visitors from all over the planet and is considered to be the greatest motorcycle sporting event in the world.

Paul told me a story once that he swears is true and I've no reason to disbelieve him. He doesn't have a tendency to exaggerate and he's told me that a million times! He was once on holiday for a few days and on his return asked his secretary if anything had happened whilst he was away.

"Nothing much", came her reply, "although a bloke from California rang to ask if we had rooms available for TT week. As if!"

"Did he give his name?"

"Yes, he said he was called Eastwood and was a motor bike fan."

"Eastwood!" screeched Paul. "And you told him we had no rooms!"

"Well, we've not! We never have any spare rooms for the TT."

"Yes, but he was called Eastwood!"

"So?"

"Did he leave a number?"

"Yes, it's on the pad on your desk."

So Paul rang the number and sure enough the Christian name of Mr. Eastwood was Clint! He offered him a suite in the Casino but fair enough to the superstar, he refused it because someone would inevitably be thrown out to accommodate him. Paul offered him a free flight and free accommodation for any other time of year but Clint said he was only interested in the motor bikes. Paul always regretted having those few days off for the publicity that was lost.

We have visited the island many, many times and always have a wonderful time. We were involved in the first three inaugural Rugby League Charity Shield games played between the winners of the league versus the cup holders. The match took place at Douglas rugby club and ended in the Lido, the famous nightclub which has long since gone. I think the competition was abandoned when Super League came into existence. We now visit the beautiful Centenary theatre in Peel during August and are treated regally by Ernie Leece and his crew!

And finally, the only person to win both the TT Race on the island and the Grand National at Aintree ....George Formby!

Nazareth House

We were just about to go on stage at the Southport theatre, when a phone rings. In most theatres you'll find a couple of telephones back stage. One is for internal calls, the other a pay phone for general use by the crew. The internal telephone was the ringing phone in question. This is used for communication between members of staff and so no outside callers are allowed through. As I pick it up I hear a wonderful Irish brogue at the other end of the phone.

"Hello, I'd like to speak to the Houghton Weavers please."

"Hello, my name's Tony, I'm one of the group", quickly realising this caller is not a member of staff.

"Hello, Tony, this is Mother Superior at Nazareth house in Blackburn."

"I'm sorry Mother but they shouldn't have put you through to this phone."

"Wonderful!"

"I'm sorry!"

"It must be a minor miracle."

"Yes, but we're about to go on stage."

"That's fine, although I'd just like to speak to you first!"

"Well you'd better hurry!"

"We've seen you all on television and we'd like you to come and sing for our residents."

"I'm afraid you'll have to speak to our office so that we can arrange a date and a fee."

"Oh, we can't pay you!"

"I'm sorry?"

"We can't pay you! We haven't any money but we thought that good Christian boys like yourselves would be only too happy to come and entertain us?"

"I'm sure it won't be a problem but as I said, we are about to go on stage so I'll ask our office to ring you back. I'm sure your number will be in the directory."

"That's fine! Please don't forget and God bless you all."

"Thanks! .....bye!" So, several days later we speak again. "Hello Tony, this is Mother Superior at Nazareth House in Blackburn. We'd love you to come and entertain our people, would that be possible?"

"I'm sure it would. Let's sort something out."

So a day is arranged for our attendance at the convent/ care home.

We arrive on the due date to be greeted by a throng of enthusiastic nuns who are all willing to help us with our equipment. Everyone appears to have a smile on their faces. We are welcomed into the lounge where all the residents are gathered. For the next hour we have a wonderful time, singing and talking to the residents and nuns. The atmosphere of the place is exceptionally welcoming and friendly and everyone appears to be at ease in their surroundings.

Following on from our concert, we are invited by the sisters into an adjacent room where food has been prepared for our benefit. Without a word of a lie, there was a bottle of "Blue Nun" wine in the centre of the spread. There was enough food for an army but it appeared that we were the only ones who were dining. The nuns are happy to sit there and watch us eat.

"Don't worry boys, we can't pay you but we can give you a feed! And don't worry, none of it will go to waste." We enjoy their company for an hour or more as they tell us about their work and enthusiastically enquire about our work. Mother Superior enquires, "You sang a song about the 'Mountain Dew', have you ever tasted any?"

"Oh, no Mother! It's illegal in this country. It's poteen or pocheen whichever way you call it and it's illegal Irish liquor!"

"Yes it is, but I don't think anybody would mind. Sister, would you please go down to the cellar and bring up the bottle marked, 'holy water'?"

I thought she was kidding but sure enough, after a few minutes the sister returned carrying a colourless bottle bearing a sticky plaster marked, 'holy water'.

"A doctor friend brought it from the mother country, would you like a little snifter?"

"What's it like?" I enquire.

"No idea! None of the sisters drink but we'd like you to have a taste.

We duly oblige and find ourselves gagging on the raw liquor.

"That's powerful stuff!"

"Oh, I'm glad you like it. Sister put some in the trifle just to give it a lift."

The trifle is just as powerful as the spirit and so, by the time we've finished the repast we are all feeling much happier than before. We left feeling that we'd done our good deed for the day but felt much better for being part of a remarkable community. We were to return many times in the future.

In the 1800s the Little Sisters of the Poor were founded by Jeanne Jugan near Rennes, in Brittany. She felt the need to care for the many elderly who lined the streets of Rennes. She originally welcomed an elderly lady into her home and so her work began. Apparently she was once seen begging in the streets of the city when a man attacked her for her audacity. She calmly replied, "You gave me that (the beating), so now give me something for the elderly." The man was so taken aback that he emptied his pockets into her collecting vessel.

The founder of the Sisters of Nazareth, Victoire Larmenier, joined the Little Sisters of the Poor some time later. After several years she was asked to found a convent in England, following a plea by the Society of St. Vincent de Paul. The first Nazareth House was built in Hammersmith in 1857. There was much uncertainty during the early years about the status of the Sisters, and in 1861, after protracted and difficult negotiations, the Holy See allowed the Hammersmith community to separate from the Little Sisters of the Poor as an independent pious society of laywomen. They began to care for children as well as the elderly. Nazareth houses are now found all over the world and Pope John Paul II stayed at Nazareth House during his visit to Manchester in 1982.

"I was a stranger and you welcomed me." Matt. 25:37

Victoire Larmenier welcomed everyone in a spirit of friendship and acceptance and we have been honoured to be part of it. They're a great bunch of women too!

This reminds me of the most frightening experience of my life! I was sitting at home one day when my mother walks into the room.

"What are you doing this afternoon?"

"Nothing, why?"

"Can you take me to Oldham? I promised I'd go and see Betty. She's just moved into a home in Oldham. I think it's a Catholic place!"

"OK, When do you want to go?"

"About two o'clock."

"Right!"

So off we go to Oldham. The old folks home is definitely Catholic because there are nuns scurrying around everywhere. One of the sisters recognises me and shouts, "Holy mother of God, it's the Houghton Weavers!"

"Yes sister. I'm here with my mother."

"Oh, it's marvellous! I'll take your mother to see Betty and then you can sing for us all."

"What?"

"I'll get the sisters together and you can sing us a few songs!"

Help! How can I get out of this!

"Well, sister, I am working tonight so I don't know whether I should."

"Wonderful! This will give you time to warm up for tonight!"

So she disappears with my mother and several minutes later she takes me into a room full of nuns. They are all sitting down in high backed, leather chairs.

"Off you go!" shouts one of them.

So I try to sing to them all, and I cannot remember when I have been as terrified in all my life! When there's a crowd of a thousand or more it isn't a problem but when you've a dozen nuns, staring at you, it becomes quite freaky!

Night Clubs

One particularly big night club in the area was "Talk of the North", in Eccles, near Manchester. We were booked to do a week and it was a relatively new adventure. At the time we wore jeans and casual shirts on stage so we generally arrived wearing our "stage" clothes.   As we were a one night stand group this was quite unusual so we were looking forward to the adventure.

We arrived on the Monday night at the front door and walked towards the pay desk.

"You can't come in here dressed like that", commented a rather large gentleman on door duty.

"It's alright!" I replied, "You don't understand. I'm one of the group who are appearing in the show!"

"Sorry, sir but it's you who doesn't understand! You can't come in here dressed like that!"

"But I'm the singer in the group."

"That's not my problem, sir", he commented, "you can't come in here dressed like that!"

"So what am I supposed to do?"

"Don't know, sir, but you're not coming in through this door!"

I wasn't going to argue too much because he was twice my size and looked rather frightening.

"Could I speak to the manager, please?" was my only solution.

"I'll give him a ring, sir, if you'll just wait over there. There are people trying to come in!"

Yeah, coming in to see me you idiot! Will I have to go home to put my suit on? Will the show go ahead? Will this giant rip me apart?

"Right sir, I've spoken to the manager and he agrees with me. You can't come in dressed like that!"

"So what am I going to do?" I ask desperately.

"The stage door is round the corner sir. If you go round there, you'll be able to go into the dressing rooms."

"And will I be able to wear these clothes on stage?"

"By all means sir. You just won't be allowed in the club."

So I walk round the corner cursing the Talk of the North and find the stage door. I'm given access to the dressing rooms and nowhere else!

So, for the rest of the week, I arrive in a suit, to gain access to the club. I then go into the changing rooms and put on my jeans to go on stage. How ridiculous! The club burned down several years later and the talk around clubland was that the bouncer wouldn't allow the firemen in to address the conflagration because they weren't dressed properly!

So here we are, sat in the changing room, waiting for the show to begin. The compere for the evening was telling gags and singing popular tunes to an ever increasing audience. We are down in the bowels of the club deciding what we are going to do on this particular night. Meanwhile a stage hand approaches us and asks if we can prepare for our entrance.

"Do we have to go up those stairs?" "No sir, the stage is there!" and points along the corridor. The stage is actually a large lift that takes us from here into the auditorium – straight up! We arrange ourselves in front of the microphones and face a brick wall! The lift then makes its way quietly up to where a packed audience is waiting on ground level. It was all quite surreal. From dingy little folk clubs to this – dingy big night clubs! The spectators, unfortunately, were more like social club crowds than theatre audiences and we had to work hard to keep the decibel levels at a reasonable height. We had had a few years apprenticeship, so we were more than able to hold our own. The stage, as I said was at ground level but there was a balcony overlooking the stage where the rabble, I mean audience, were able to hang from the gallery and heckle. I imagine it to be quite similar to a Roman amphitheatre, we

105

being the Christians who had just been thrown to the lions! It certainly kept you on your toes! There could be no more than a second of dithering or they would attack!

I had far more experience of noisy audiences as I had worked in social clubs as a solo act before the Weavers were formed. The other lads hated the noise so I had to remind them that we were getting well paid, so live with it! So, although we didn't particularly enjoy it, we lived with it!

Denis had moved his amplifier to the edge of the stage so that he had more room to move around. The audience were noisy but appeared to be enjoying the night. That couldn't be said for David and Norman as they worked their way, tediously through the show. Fortunately, we were only on stage for one set of about an hour. The time went slowly by as we reached our finale and to our surprise, the "lift" began its long way to the basement. The audience, who by now, were well topped up with alcohol, were cheering for more as we slowly descended. As our heads became level with ground level, I suddenly realised that Denis' amp was still on the lip of the stage and his guitar was still plugged in.................too late! It suddenly decided that gravity was the best option and fell into the chasm, just missing the members of the group and a stage hand who had come to clear our gear from the stage!

We endured the week but decided that night clubs were not to be our forte and so that was to be our first and last visit. It was very fortuitous that we enjoyed theatres in preference to night clubs and social clubs, as the former have improved beyond recognition and the latter have all but completely disappeared.

London

We are invited to do another pantomime in Blackpool at the fabulous Grand Theatre. It's all agreed and we find that our producer will be Freddie Davies. Freddie was an act in his own right and was called 'parrot face'. He did a sketch about a budgie and the name stuck. Stuck that much that he did a telly advert for 'Trill' budgie food, with the caption, 'Trill makes budgies bounce with health'. He also did an advert for a Blackburn brewery which went, 'Thwaites thtout is thmashing!'

He decided that we should go down to London to rehearse for the show which we duly did. We arrived early on the Monday morning and were introduced to the rest of the cast. We were to rehearse in the 'Pineapple' studios in London for a week. We needed more rehearsals than most, as none of us were fully au fait with the work of a thespian! We were especially in need of dance training because a couple of the group were blessed with two left feet.

After rehearsals, we went out together for a meal. Each night we each had a turn in choosing what type of food we would eat. We tried French, English, Italian and finally Chinese. On arrival at the restaurant I asked the waiter what type of soup was on the menu.

He replied, "Soup, oh, cluck, cluck, cluck!"

I said, "Chicken?"

"No mushroom," came his reply.

"Why did you make a noise like a chicken?" I countered.

"Because I can't make a noise like a mushroom!"

107

The meal went well and there was plenty of it but as the saying goes, an hour after a Chinese meal, you begin to feel hungry again!

We decided to wander the streets near our hotel and came across a kebab house. It was getting rather late but we were all feeling a bit peckish, so we entered the establishment. A bit 'greasy spoon', but at that time of night it didn't matter. I ordered a kebab and the server asked if I would like pepper sauce. I'd never tried it before but I thought, "Why not? When in Rome."

As we walked down the street munching on my supper, I realised that this pepper sauce was the hottest thing I'd ever tasted in my life! We arrived back in our hotel and a couple of pints of bitter helped to cool my burning throat. I could feel it corroding my stomach as it slowly went down. I began to flush as the blistering sauce made its way through my innards.

The following morning we had arranged to go down to Freddie's costume department to be fitted with our outfits. I have never been more embarrassed in my life, as my supper began to churn away in my guts and everyone was singing the Johnny Cash hit, 'Ring of Fire'. I spent most of the morning on the toilet and tried to steer clear of all and sundry!

It was arranged that we would not rehearse on Friday morning, so that we could make our way home during the quieter part of the day. We were all packed and ready for the more serious rehearsals at the theatre the following week.

"Before we leave", asked David, "Could we go and see Soho? I've never been before and whilst we are so close!"

"We'll just have a little walk down but we're not stopping anywhere!" says Norman.

"That's OK, just a peak!" According to the 'Visit London' website;

Soho was developed as an urban area from the late 16th century onwards. The name Soho is thought to come from a 17th century hunting and battle cry. From the 17th to the early 20th century Soho was avoided by its rich neighbours in Bloomsbury and Mayfair and the area developed a reputation for prostitution, music halls, cheap food and shady dealings. During the 20th century it became the centre of bohemian London with intellectuals, writers, artists and poets eating and drinking in the many pubs and restaurants. Beatnik culture began here and Carnaby Street was a centrepiece for the' swinging sixties'. Soho today has shed its seedy reputation although there are still burlesque shows to retain its risqué vibe.

And that was what we were here for! The risqué vibe! Well! boys will be boys! So nervously we wandered through the passages, holding on to our baggage for dear life. It was quite seedy and I certainly didn't want to stay long. This was something I'd never seen in my life before. A good Catholic lad who lives with his mum! Then we heard,

"Come in boys and see the show!"

"It's only 10 o'clock in the morning!"

"Great shows all day boys!"

"No thanks!"

"Should we have a go?" asks David.

"Well how much will it cost?"

"I'll go and ask! Excuse me, but how much is it to come in?"

"Forty shillings! Stay as long as you like!" came the reply. "Forty shillings? It's not been shillings for ten years!"

"Two quid then mate! Are you from oop North?"

"Yes, Manchester!" I state

"Well, are we going in?" asks David

"I don't think I fancy it!" retorts Norman

"This is probably the only time in your life you'll see anything like this", says David.

"Like what?" I counter.

"Well we'll have to go in to find that out!"

"Take a vote!" suggests Norman, "stay or go?" I'll not tell you who voted what but the majority said 'stay'! So our treasurer for the day pays forty shillings each to a bloke that would make the Kray twins nervous. He leads us through a curtain and down a steep flight of stairs. We stand in front of the curtain until a young lad steps through the folds and says, "Forty shillings each please!"

"But we've just paid forty shillings to Quasi Modo, upstairs!"

"Yes sir, that's membership! You need to pay forty shillings each to come in!"

"Treasurer! Pay the man!"

So our treasurer, David, forks out more money to the young lad.

He leads us through the curtain, into a darkened room where we could make out tables and chairs through the gloom. He walks right through this room and goes through another curtain, up a flight of stairs and we are back in the street!

"Follow me!" and he sets off at a fairly rapid pace.

"Don't let him out of your sights!" screams Denis, "He's probably the Greek 100 metres champion!"

We follow this lad for about two hundred yards until we arrive at a similar type of establishment to the one we've just left.

The boy gives our tickets to the man on the door who looks us all up and down and states, "Morning boys! Forty shillings, stay as long as you like!"

"Forty bloody shillings! We've paid that twice, we're not paying again!"

"Forty shillings boys or you don't come in!"

"I'll bloody kill him!" shouts Denis.

"Denis, don't be stupid! Have you seen those gorillas behind him?"

"Well, maybe not! So what are we going to do?"

"Well it's another forty shillings or we cut our losses and go home!"

So we did the latter and, tails between our legs, we never saw the sights of Soho!

Keeping fit

I had begun to regularly attend the local fitness club in an attempt to gain some of the fitness that I had acquired as a P.E. student a few years before. I'd play squash regularly, train three or four times a week, go swimming and play the occasional game of five a side football. One thing I hated was running! I'd try it for twenty minutes or so on a running machine but despised going out in the countryside for a jog. I had to force myself to take to the road but eventually I reached a reasonable degree of fitness.

I began to drive to the countryside, then have a run round the moorlands, just to look at the scenery, which would take my mind off the tedious drudgery called running! The fact that every game I played required one to run constantly never took away from the fact that I could never get used to just running! I would play squash with other group members, especially Norman, on a regular basis. We both disliked losing and it was a major battle every time we took to the court. We were fairly evenly matched which made the competition even more interesting. Many people watching would comment that it appeared that the murder of the opponent was more preferable than losing! Keeping fit has occupied the attention of many thinkers over the years. Thousands of years ago it wasn't as necessary as today to keep fit because the hunter gatherer was running, walking, and generally keeping fit without thinking about it. However, the ancient Greeks took fitness very seriously. They did invent the Olympic Games for example.

The care of health begins the moment a man wakes up. After awakening he should not arise at once but should wait until the heaviness of sleep has gone. Then, every day, he should wash his face and eyes using pure water. He should rub his teeth using some fine peppermint powder and taking away any leftover bits of food. He should rub and anoint his head every day but wash it and comb it only occasionally.

After this, people who have to or wish to work will do so, but people of leisure will first take a walk. A young man or middle-aged man should take a walk of about 10 stadia before sunrise. Long walks before meals clear out the body, prepare it for food and give it more power for digesting.

Hippocrates, 'Regimen' (c.500BC)

During one of the television shows, I remember taking my pulse when we arrived at the studio. It was a very normal sixty beats per minute. As the day went on, I continued to check my pulse and as show time approached my pulse was getting faster and faster until just before we were introduced on stage, when it had gone to an incredible one hundred and twenty! Now that sort of tempo would only be reached with quite strenuous physical activity normally but the expectation of being in front of the television cameras had set it racing! Is that what they call adrenaline?

A woman sees an elderly man sitting on a park bench. He looks ever so happy, so the woman sits next to him and asks, "What's your secret for a happy life?"

The guy replies, "I smoke 60 fags a day, drink a dozen pints of beer every night, eat lots of fatty foods and never exercise!"

"That's amazing!" comments the woman, "And just how old are you?"

The man smiles and replies, "Twenty seven!"

Surprisingly It's Spring!

Everything was going tremendously well and bookings were coming in thick and fast. We were into our third series on BBC when Terry Wheeler rang for a chat.

"Hello, Tony, how's it going?"

"Fine thanks! What can I do for you?"

"Well, I've just devised a new show that I'm going to call 'Surprisingly it's Spring!' and, after chatting to my bosses, they think it would be great if you hosted the show and sang a couple of songs on each. What do you think?"

"My goodness Terry, I'm quite taken aback! Thanks for asking and I'd certainly love to do it. But before I say a definite 'yes' I think I'd better run it past the group just in case they object. I'm sure there won't be a problem but I think that it's only etiquette, don't you?"

"Absolutely! There's no rush. Nothing will be done for at least three or four weeks, so I'll hear from you soon?"

"Definitely, and thanks for asking."

My goodness! Solo! There are millions of singers in the North West and he has asked me! Incredible! The lads will be really pleased for me – it will give the group a load of extra publicity.

How wrong I was!

Thus began several weeks of animosity with my fellow 'Weavers'. We'd never had more than a tiff about material on stage but this started a full blown row!

"You can't do it!"

"What do you mean, I can't do it!"

"You just can't do it!"

"Why not? It will only give the group more publicity, which can only be good!"

"But if it goes well, you'll leave the group!"

"Don't be bloody stupid, of course I won't!"

"Well, I don't think you should do it. What do you think, Denis, David?"

"I agree with Norman, you'll only leave the group if it goes well!"

"For God sake! Have you no faith in me when I say I have no intention of leaving the group! I started the group in the first place because I hated working solo!"

And so the arguments continued for the next few days and I was beginning to think that a solo career might not be a bad thing. *At least I wouldn't have to go through all this crap! What started off as a wonderful idea was beginning to split the group!*

After several days of stonewalling by both parties I got a phone call from Norman.

"We'd like to get together to discuss your possible appearance on Terry's new show."

"Yeah, where?"

"We'll meet at my house tomorrow morning."

Meet at his house eh? Every time we meet it's at the pub so they must need a venue where they will have the upper hand!

"What's wrong with the Red Lion?"

"I think it would be better to meet at my house, say 10.30?"

"OK, I'll see you there."

So, for the rest of the day I work out my strategy. Should I just bow down to their objections and refuse to do the show or should I stick up for myself and tell them where to go?

No, why should I. The only reason they don't want me to do it is for utterly selfish reasons. Then again, why do I want to do it?.......... for utterly selfish reasons? I really want to do the show, so unless they can come up with a better reason than leaving the group, I'll just tell them where to stick it! We've known each other long enough – can they not trust me?

So the following morning arrives and I turn up at Norman's house where the 'jury' are sitting in discussion of the 'traitor' for that's what it felt like!

"Well," I begin, "I think it's a great opportunity and I'd love to do the show. I have absolutely no intention of leaving the group and I thought you would have trusted me when I told you that was my intention. I'm not here to argue with you all but my mind is made up!"

"Well, as spokesman," Norman begins, "we really do not want you to do the programme but realise that your mind is set so we've agreed a compromise!"

"A compromise is when both parties meet in the middle, so how can you have reached a compromise if I don't know what's been agreed!"

"Now let's not get pedantic! What we suggest is that you do the show, but all monies that you get will be put into the 'Weavers' account."

"Why do you want my money? I'll be earning it so why should I give it to you? It's not fair and you know it but if it clears the air then I'll agree but I need to have a think about it first."

So that was almost that! I could do the show with their acceptance rather than approval. I'm not too sure about the money though! It's not the financial benefits I'm worried about but the fact that they want to control me which I don't like!

So I ring Terry Wheeler and say that I'm available for the show should he still need me. "Of course, we still need you! I'll send the contract through the post in the next few days. Thanks again!"

Several days later I receive the BBC contract through the post informing me that for the seven shows I would receive £350. Not a fortune but a considerable amount of money for the late 70s. I'll get the money some time during the recording of the show and transfer it to the Weavers bank account! *Weavers bank account! Why should they get all the money while I've done all the work? It is not the money at all but the principle behind it!*

Then a gem of an idea springs into my subconscious! I wonder if they'll fall for it? It's worth a try.

During the next few days we were rehearsing in the upstairs room in the Red Lion when I broach the subject.

"Alright gents? You know this 'Surprisingly it's Spring' thing? I know I have to give the money to the group but do you think it would be possible to buy a few items of clothes out of the money and pass the remainder on to you. You see, I'll need a few new shirts if I'm going to look OK."

"What do you think boys? Should we let him have a few shirts?"

"I think that would be OK – go ahead!"

OK! Go ahead! It's my bloody money and here they are telling me what I should do with it!

"Thanks a lot!"

So the next day, I went into Bolton and spent exactly £350 on clothes! I didn't want or need the clothes I just felt so angry that they were trying to control me but more importantly that they didn't trust me! And it did make me feel a lot better!

So the show went ahead and if nothing else, I was the smartest singer on the programme! Hostilities amongst the group soon died down and everything returned to normal for the time being. We were so much like a family – in each others' pockets for many, many hours each week, so that arguments were impossible to avoid but we didn't do too badly considering everything.

Mons

Southport theatre asked if we would consider doing the summer season there during the months of June to September. We accepted and worked there every Friday night for many years throughout the summer. We occasionally brought a guest to entertain the crowds. Howard Broadbent, writer of several songs that we were singing at the time, was one of these such guests. We'd met him several years before and he'd sent us numerous tapes of songs that he'd written which impressed us very much. So much so, that the BBC commissioned him to write a set of songs for one of our upcoming series on the BBC. Howard was asked to write seven songs so that we could feature one in each of the shows. A marvellous character, Howard was a highly proficient golfer and appeared in the 'Open' golf championship on two occasions. His songs generally told of the town of his birth, Bolton, or of his political beliefs. Politics was a highly volatile subject during the late 70's and 80's when Margaret Thatcher changed the face of Britain forever with her highly contentious political views. She argued, in her early days in power, that her friends around her advised her, especially William Whitelaw and once, tongue in cheek said, "Every cabinet needs a Willy!" It didn't take long before she ignored the advice of all around her and went her own way. Her eventual downfall came when she introduced the Community Charge or 'Poll Tax', causing riots in the streets of Britain. Only 12% of the population surveyed agreed with this system of tax and, following Thatcher's resignation, the new Prime Minister, John Major, abolished it and replaced it with the Council Tax.

Going back to Southport! We were approached by the theatre manager, Phil King, and asked if we'd like to accompany a delegation from Southport, to visit their twinned town of Mons in Belgium. It was our first foray abroad and so we jumped at the idea. We were to travel by coach from Southport to Plymouth, then take the ferry to Zeebrugge and on to Mons. The party consisted of ourselves, local dignitaries, catering staff and a Morris dancing troupe! We were to do a show in Mons Town Hall and the catering staff would cook a meal for the gathered crowd.

We arrived in Southport on the morning of our departure to be greeted by the Morris dancers, strutting their stuff on the promenade! Very ethnic! I've nothing against Morris dancers but it's not a hobby that I would pursue! However, many people do and it dates back to at least the 15th century when records showed that the Goldsmiths Company paid seven shillings to be entertained by a troupe of Morris dancers. And we were getting it for free!

Once everyone was on board, we departed on a very circuitous route to Plymouth. All conversation was centred around the show we would be putting on the next day. The audience were going to be fed Lancashire hotpot, black puddings and mushy peas by the chefs on board and given a truly Lancashire evening of entertainment by our Morris dancers and folk from the Houghton Weavers.

Is this going to work? Will they understand a word we are singing, or even more to the point, a word we are saying? This could be an unmitigated disaster or a surreal experience for all!

We stopped a couple of times for a brew and something to eat, whilst Phil King entertained all on board with his wit. Phil was the organiser of the event and also the manager of the Southport theatre complex. He was always ready with a witty comment and can still be heard today as he is the entertainment writer for the Southport Visitor. He is an absolute mine of information as regards the entertainment industry and can regularly be seen with a flock of people hanging on his every word. He explained that everything would be alright even though they would be a French

118

audience, "It could be worse", he commented, "they could all be Walloons!"

By the time we arrived in Belgium I had had more than my fair share of showbiz gossip and the intricacies of the Morris, mumming and pace egging plays! All I fancied was a beer but unfortunately they don't make the type of beer that I like. Theirs is made by the Trappist monks who must have been permanently sozzled as they made their tremendously strong brews. A few hundred years ago it was much more preferential to drink beer than to drink water as it could be quite toxic. I think I might be from that era?

We had a walk round the square and looked in at the various museums before preparing ourselves for the evening. Mons is a beautiful city but has had its fair share of turmoil. The first battle fought by British troops in the First World War took place here and there is a plaque in the entrance to the city hall that tells us..... "After fifty months of German occupation freedom was restored to the city. Here was fired the last shot of the Great War...." Mons was also heavily bombed during the Second World War as it was an important industrial centre.

The main emblem of Mons is a monkey who sits on its haunches. The origin of the monkey is lost in the mists of time but there is a tradition that when you walk past the statue that graces the entrance to the City Hall you should touch its head with your hand to grant yourself a wish.

Another legend that sprung from the First World War is that of the Mons 'Angels'. On the 22nd and 23rd August 1914 the first action involving British troops began in the town. The British troops were vastly outnumbered by the German forces but managed to hold them back for quite a while longer than would have been expected. Shortly afterwards, upon reading of the exploits of the troops, a Welsh author named Arthur Macken, published a short fictional story describing bowmen from the battle of Agincourt who had come to help these troops following a prayer by one of the soldiers to St. George. Many people did not read the 'fictional' bit in the story and began to believe that this was a miracle. The bowmen became Angels of Mercy in people's eyes which caused Macken to eventually write had succeeded..... "I had succeeded unwittingly in the art of deceit....the snowball of rumour that was then set rolling has been rolling ever since, growing bigger and bigger till it is now swollen to a monstrous size!....."

So we arrived at the Town Hall and set up all our equipment. Everyone was running around in a panic preparing for our Belgian guests. Slowly they began to trickle in and, following a few glasses of beer or wine, everyone began to relax. Maybe everything would be OK after all. The starters were beginning to be served and one or two eyebrows were raised. It didn't look good when these well dressed dignitaries began to push their black puddings to the sides of the plates and asked if they could have another piece of bread with French, not English mustard! They then began enquiring as to the type of meat in their hot pot and wondered if the mushy peas were meant to be eaten or were just decoration! Lots of almost full plates were being returned to the kitchen with shakes of the head. The only thing going down well was the wine! Next, they had to endure half an hour of 'the Morris'. The dancers had begun to get nervous as they sensed that things weren't going to plan. The squire, who introduces the dances, was having trouble with his French pronunciation whilst the 'bagman', the 'ragman', the 'foreman', the 'fool' and the 'hobby' were struggling to keep in step with each other. Thirty minutes is a long time when nobody appears to be enjoying what you are doing but eventually it came to an end.

Then it was our turn!

"Bugger it! Let's just do what we do and if they don't like it then it's understandable!"

So we did what we do and they quite liked it! I'm sure they couldn't understand the jokes but when I opened my mouth they just laughed anyway. We sang our full range of raucous songs, a few poignant, a few ballads and a couple of humorous ones which all went down quite well; if fact, very well indeed, so we rescued what could have been an unmitigated disaster.

At the end of the show, the mayor of Mons presented each of us with a copy of the Mons monkey, which I still have to this day. Then a gentleman stood up to give a vote of thanks.

"My Lord Mayor, distinguished guests, ladies and gentlemen; I'd like to thank you for coming this evening. I'd like to thank our chefs and their staff for the interesting Lancashire fayre"; ripple of laughter and subdued applause, "I'd like to thank our dancers who gave us some remarkable footwork", more polite applause, "And finally I'd like to express a tremendous amount of gratitude to the Houghton Weavers. I have been Professor of English at Mons University for the past twenty-five years and after listening to their show for the past hour, I realise that I have been using the wrong dictionary!"

This brought the house down! Everyone relaxed; we had several more glasses of wine and reflected on a marvellous evening of cross border bon homie! It's not what you do; it's the way that you do it!

A television channel in America once rang the British Ambassador and asked him what he'd like for the New Year. He answered, "I'm not allowed to accept gifts in my position but maybe a small box of chocolates might be nice?"

A couple of nights later on that channel the newscaster announced that several statesmen had been asked what they would like for the New Year. "The German Member of Parliament has asked for world peace and the French Minister suggested that obliterating world poverty would be tremendous, whilst the English Ambassador said that he'd like a box of chocolates!"

Shades of Blue

If I was free from the Weavers, I sometimes joined forces with some of my friends and formed a group of entertainers. There was a drummer, Kevin, a pianists, George and Phil, guitarists, David, Mike and my brother James. The best magician in Westhoughton, John, singer and the funniest man in the world, Tom. We usually did charity shows in our area and raised lots of money for various good causes whilst having a whale of a time ourselves. A couple of hours were never enough to accommodate the half a dozen egos that wanted to show off their various talents. Not that any of them were big-headed; on the contrary, they were the nicest bunch of blokes you could ever wish to meet.

George suggested we all wore black trousers and blue shirts but on our first gig we all turned up in different shades of blue shirts, hence the name. Following several nights on the road we changed our name to 'The Odds and Sods' because it was always a different line-up.

On one particular occasion we were working in Chorley, at a residential centre for adults with learning difficulties. Mike, one of our guitarists, turned up with a stunning blonde who called herself Bernadette. "She's a clients daughter and would like to become an Odd or Sod", he said.

"So what do you play, Bernadette?"

"Nothing", came her reply.

"So do you sing?"

"Not really."

"So what are you going to do?" I ask.

"She doesn't have to do anything!" chortles David, "She can just stand by me and look gorgeous!"

"She'll have to pretend to do something", I counter. "Maybe you could play tambourine?"

"OK, fine!" comes her reply.

We find a tambourine in the bottom of Kevin's bag of tricks and the Odds and Sods watch open mouthed as our new member attempts to play her musical instrument.

"Let me show you how to hold it," giggles David with a lecherous look on his face.

The banter continues and Bernadette woos everyone with her looks and absolutely nobody with her musical abilities. The gig goes well but nobody can remember a thing about it; all talk is about our new recruit.

"She's an absolutely beautiful creature but she's a typical dumb blonde," was the general opinion.

"She'll get by on her looks. She doesn't need a brain."

So that was the end of that until a few weeks later when I was perusing our Sunday newspaper. I turn over a page and there she is looking at me with a headline, 'Clive Sinclair get's engaged to someone brainier than himself!' It goes on to say........Bernadette, with an IQ of 154, two more than Sir Clive....... How wrong can you be! We'd all assumed this glorious creature was a bit thick but the newspaper article refuted that in no uncertain terms. I don't think they ever got married but I think she'll be able to cope; good luck Bernadette! We never saw her again!

EMI Christmas Party

We were invited by EMI to entertain the workforce at their annual Christmas party. It was to take place at the Heathrow Airport Hotel in the capital. In conversation with their hierarchy, it seemed that it wouldn't create too much of a problem if I brought a friend and called them a 'helper'. Following discussions over a pint, it was obvious that a couple of my friends would love to join us for the weekend. It was agreed with the rest of the lads that Frankie and Kev Mac would become extra roadies on our escapade.

We met early on the Friday morning and had a leisurely and extremely enjoyable drive down to London. All talk was of the impending weekend. We were about to entertain the workforce of one of the biggest recording agencies in the world and Frankie and Kev Mac had every intention of having a good weekend!

"How are we going to entertain people who've seen and heard everything?"

"Just be ourselves! It's worked in the past."

"Yeah, but we aren't singing to Lancashire folk, we're singing to the bosses of EMI."

"Don't worry, they are just the same as everybody else, except they're from south of Watford!"

"Will there be a bar at this place?" chirps Frankie.

"Don't worry, if they work for EMI they probably like a drink!"

"What songs should we sing?" "We'd better put a couple in from our new album." "Yeah, but don't forget the Lancashire songs, that's why they signed us up in the first place."

"Will the drinks be expensive?"

"Shouldn't be; we are only in the nation's capital and singing at Heathrow airport! Of course it'll be expensive!"

"Frankie, don't worry, we'll find a nice friendly face and let them buy you drinks all night."

"Might be a free bar if you're lucky!"

"Never mind the bar, what are we going to sing?" And so it continues light heartedly until we arrive at Heathrow airport. We all disappear to our rooms as we have a few hours to kill.

"I'll have a read and a shower; see you around six in the foyer."

"Me and Frankie will be in the bar!" shouts Kev.

"Let's all meet in the bar at six, so we can have a sound check and run through a few numbers."

So that was agreed. I make my way to the room to have a lie down. An hour or two later I can hear a commotion as Kev and Frankie are having a bit of a row.

"Just put your key in and the door should open!" shouts Frankie.

"I've tried that but it won't work!" counters Kev.

I go to the corridor to find them in deep conversation.

"What's the problem?"

"Well every room has a bar and we've emptied Frankie's but I can't get into mine!"

"Let's have a go." So I try without much success to open the room bar/fridge. I come into the corridor and see a young woman coming my way. She's obviously a chambermaid and so I call to Kev, "Have a word with this young lady, she may be able to help."

"Well love, the problem is my bar."

"What's wrong with your bar, sir?"

"I can't get into it, that's the problem!"

"Don't worry sir, just call reception and tell them that your 'Captain Bell' isn't working.

"Thanks love!"

I then overhear a surreal one sided conversation as Kev rings reception.

"Hello, love, it's Kev in room 232. I've just been talking to the landlady and she's told me to tell you that Captain Cook isn't working."

Pause, then Kev continues, "Landlady, yes, she had a blue frock on and a badge that said Susan!"

Pause, "Captain Cook! I can't open him!" pause, "Well Captain Bell then. It doesn't really matter what it's called love, I only want a drink!"

Eventually he puts the phone down to see me and Frankie in fits of laughter.

"She's sending somebody up to mend it! I think I'll have a sleep till tea time."

So everyone retires to their room until early evening when we go down to the ballroom to sort our show out. Once the sound check is complete, we go back upstairs to dress for dinner.

On returning to the ballroom an hour later, the place is beginning to fill up. There are people of every colour, creed and size. Each one showing their individuality to the world! What a cross section of unusualness! We felt very intimidated because we looked so ordinary. People were arriving in bright pink dress suits, others in ripped jeans and tea shirts, whilst we had been told to wear dinner suits.

"What's going on, they're all nutters!" retorts Kev.

"Where have you brought us, Legs!" counters Frankie. Forgot to tell you, 'Legs' was my nickname!

"Don't worry", I reply, "Let's go over and see Bob and Vic".

That's not Bob Mortimer and Vic Reeves but Bob and Vic from EMI. Bob Barratt produced all three of our EMI recordings including the one we did at Abbey Road whilst Vic was his boss. He was head of MOR for the company. MOR, or Middle of the Road included artists such as Cliff Richard, Shirley Bassey and the like, so he was a big cheese!

"Well hello, boys!" "Howdo! Vic" "How's everything going with you four?" "Fine thanks, Vic". "I see you've got a couple of extras with you this evening.

So who are these strapping young gentlemen?"

"This is Frankie and Kev".

"Well Frankie and Kev, would you like to join me at the bar for a drink whilst these boys entertain us all?"

"Too right!" says Frankie, and whispers in Kev's ear, "Don't let this bloke out of you sight for the rest of the night.

He's got a wad of twenty pound notes in his pocket that would strangle a cat!"

"He's gay, Frankie!"

"I couldn't give a toss if he's Danny La bloody Rue if he gets the drinks in all night!"

So we leave Vic with his new companions and take to the stage. It's not much different than at home in a situation like this. Corporate nights tend to be very much the same. The vast majority of the audience are more concerned with doing business than listening to the artists. However, we get reasonable attention and the hour flies by very quickly indeed. To a decent round of applause we finish our work for the evening and rejoin the others in the lounge.

On entry, I see Kev and Frankie in deep conversation with Vic, who appears to be having a whale of a time. They are sitting around a table full of empty glasses and everyone seems to be blissfully content.

"Come and join us boys, I'm having a marvellous time with Frankie and Kev. Get a drink from the bar and charge it to my room."

"That's a bit dangerous Vic, with those two around!"

"Nonsense, we're having a marvellous time! By the way Frankie, I never asked if you're in the music industry?"

Frankie was an engineer (that is mechanical engineer not musical engineer) and couldn't sing a note in tune and had never touched a musical instrument of any sort, although he used to put his pint pot down on the piano at the Red Lion.

"Oh yes Vic, I've been in the music industry for quite a few years!"

"What do you do?" enquires Vic enthusiastically.

"Well, Kev and me are a double act! I play the fiddle and Kev is a fantastic Irish dancer!"

"Oh my God! What's he doing! We're going to lose our EMI contract if he doesn't stop it!"

"And where do you work? In the Manchester area?"

"All over the North of England, although we're trying to get some gigs round here. We've been support for the Weavers on some of their bigger gigs, Free Trade Hall, Guild Hall, Pier Head at Liverpool."

"So, have you got a name?"

127

"Oh aye, we're called 'Fiddle and Clog'; you might have heard of us?"

"Fiddle and Clog, eh? It does ring a bell. I'll have to come up north to take a look at you or maybe I could ask some agent friends of mine to get you a gig!"

"Well done Vic, that would be great! Do you want Kev to give you a twirl?"

This is getting ridiculous! I'm going to have to do something.

"I don't think Kev's in the right frame of mind to start dancing at this time of night. He needs an hour to warm up doesn't he?" I plead.

Frankie's really enjoying this, "No, he'll be alright! I'll go up to my room to get my fiddle and we can have a bit of a 'do' in the foyer!"

"I don't think that's wise Frankie, Kev's had a few too many. Maybe tomorrow?"

"What a good idea, Tony, tomorrow it is! After breakfast you can give us a twirl! Meanwhile, I think it's time I left you good people, it's a bit past my bedtime."

"OK, Vic, see you in the morning!"

So Vic minces his way towards the lift but not before he blows Frankie a kiss!

"I'll bloody kill you, Frankie!"

"What's wrong, Legs? He'd have loved to see Kev strutting his stuff! Maybe he'll get us a few gigs down here?"

"My God Keith, you must have had a few, you're beginning to believe it yourself!"

Kev, who had, by this time fallen asleep, began to snore in his armchair. Frankie leans over and gives him a shake, "Let's have one more before we call it a day".

Fortunately, we didn't see Vic at the breakfast table in the morning and so we left London with our reputation intact whilst Frankie and Kev snored all the way home! I often wonder if he made any enquiries about getting them a job in London!

Another Frankie

Another Frankie was my idol. Frank Worthington played for Bolton Wanderers between 1977 and 1979 and in 84 appearances for the Trotters scored 35 goals. He was always a joy to watch and appeared to enjoy his football; not bad for a tyke! (He was born in Shelf near Halifax). In his second season at Bolton he was leading goal scorer in the top flight of English football even though Bolton finished fourth from bottom and only just avoided relegation.

Westhoughton staged an open cup competition every year for charity. The president of the cup committee was Francis, or 'Franny' Lee, a local legend, who played for Bolton, Manchester City, Derby County and England. The Charity cup which started in 1893 and was won in that year by Westhoughton Olympic, was organised by the co-operative friendly society to help members in need. The cup went into decline after the war and eventually out of existence. In 1969 it was revived by locals and Franny was brought on board. The final would take place at Daisy Hill football club and Franny would bring a famous footballing personality to the contest to judge the 'Man of the Match'. I remember the likes of Peter Reid, Mike Summerbee and Malcolm Allison adjudicating but "Franky, Franky, Franky, Franky Worthington" was the zenith!

I was asked to commentate to the crowds on several occasions but this particular day would be a highlight. To do the announcing I would borrow a small sound system from a friend and tell the crowds what was going on. "The bar's over there, the toilets are over there and there are crisps available behind the bar!" (Daisy Hill is not exactly Wembley!)

It was a popular competition and regularly drew a crowd around the one thousand mark but on this special event they seemed more numerous than normal. When Franny and Frankie arrived, hoards of youngsters crowded the Wanderers favourite for his autograph. Keith Riley, an old footballing team mate of mine, shepherded the crowds aside and commented, "Don't worry lads, Frank will give autographs after the match. He's needed to judge the Man of the Match, so leave him alone till then!"

There was muttering from the older spectators. "Like hell he will, Prima donna!"

"You're right, two minutes after they've finished he'll be off!"

"They all get paid too much anyway, it's the least he could do!"

This is my hero they are talking about! I just hope they're not right.

So the match begins and turned out be quite an exciting affair. There were several goals but I remember little else. At the conclusion of the game, cups and medals are presented by the guest of honour and, as the crowds begin to disperse Keith approaches Franny and Frank.

"Gents, there's food and drink at the Conservative club if you're ready to leave."

"You'll have to hang on Keith; I promised these lads an autograph!"

And so my hero spent almost an hour giving personal messages and his autograph to every single one of them! My only regret was that the blokes who were calling him names earlier had disappeared to the bar. What a great bloke and a great footballer. I still remember that goal against Ipswich!

Football

I'm still watching the mighty Bolton Wanderers at this time but because we are reasonably well known, we get asked to join several celebrity football and cricket and even basketball matches. Bolton Wanderers, for a couple of seasons, had a sister sport with the same name. Bolton Wanderers launched a basketball team. They played at the Leisure Centre at Horwich and to launch the season's first game they had a warm up match featuring members of the current Wanderers first team and many celebrity footballers from Manchester United, Liverpool, Everton and yours truly! What a chaotic evening that was but I loved every minute of it; playing with my sporting heroes. I played many celebrity football matches and quite a few cricket games and even got to speak to some of these sporting greats.

We were regularly asked to attend Sporting 'dinners' where a personality would give a talk about his or her career and would be followed by a local comedian. The first time I asked anybody for their autograph was at one such event when a special the guest for the evening was the legendary Dixie Dean.

Born, William Ralph Dean in 1907, the same year as my dad, he began his footballing career at Tranmere Rovers. He later moved to Everton, the club he supported as a lad, and became a sporting legend. In the 1927-28 season, he scored 60 league goals, a feat that has never been equalled. At the age of 32, he signed for Sligo Rovers in the Irish league, scoring 10 goals in seven games. One of those was in the Irish Cup final but the match finished in a draw and Shelbourne won the replay. Dixie's runner-up medal was stolen from his hotel room. Thirty-nine years later when he attended the Irish Cup final as guest of honour, a package was delivered to his hotel containing the said medal.

He was once asked if his greatest achievement would ever be bettered. Dean said, "People ask me if that 60-goal record will ever be beaten. I think it will. But there's only one man who'll do it. That's the fellow that walks on the water. I think he's about the only one."

On his death, the great Bill Shankly said, "He belongs to the company of the supremely great, like Beethoven, Shakespeare and Rembrandt!" But my favourite story about Dixie Dean happened before he came to international fame. Whilst playing for Tranmere Rovers he was on the receiving end of a tough challenge which resulted in him losing a testicle in a reserve game against Altrincham. Immediately following the challenge, a teammate rubbed the area to ease the pain. Dean shouted "Don't rub 'em, count 'em!"

My other footballing anecdote from this time tells of another legendary Everton footballer, Duncan McKenzie. He only played there for two seasons and scored 14 goals. He was born in the same year as me and besides playing for many teams in the English league he has played for Anderlecht in Belgium, Tulsa Roughnecks in the USA and Ryoden FC in Hong Kong. Besides being a talismanic player Duncan also attracted publicity by being able to throw a golf ball the length of a football pitch and his ability to jump over a stationary 'Mini'. He related to me one evening, "In those days I was earning £12 a week from Everton but people would give me £10 for jumping over a Mini. It got to the point where, if I jumped over two cars in a week, I was earning more money than when I played in front of 40,000 on a Saturday afternoon!" Nowadays, to earn an extra crust, I think Wayne Rooney would have to jump over a Ferrari, or a Lamborghini, don't you think? Then again, I think he earns a bit more than £12 a week!

Knott End

We'd got a booking in Pilling, on the Fylde coast and it was a beautiful day so I thought I'd invite a girl out for the day.

So my mother and I set off for a drive around the area before the gig! She had friends in the area and had agreed to join them for the evening. I took the top off the car and took a very leisurely drive to the country. My mother was enjoying the ride and I suggested we might eat.

"There's a cafe on the front at Knott End, we could go there. I'll treat you to your dinner."

"Thanks a lot! No expense spent!"

"What's that love, I can't hear you with the wind blowing."

"Nothing; I didn't say a word! Knott End it is then!" It is not clear how Knott End got its name. One theory is that the "knotts" were two large mounds of stones which lay out in the river until they were destroyed in the construction of the entrance to the Wyre Dock. Others believe that the name may have been derived from the 'knot', a bird that frequents the sands of Morecambe Bay. Knott End is situated to the south of the bay whilst the other boundary is the River Wyre. Another thought is that, when entering the estuary, the early Norse seafarers used knotted ropes as navigational tools - the knots marking distance with Knott End being at the end of the rope.

The area has been occupied for centuries, even as far back as the Stone Age. The main source of work being the land and the sea; farming and fishing. That is until the middle of the 19th century when borings were taken in the hope of finding iron ore. Sadly, that proved ineffectual but vast quantities of rock salt were discovered. This became the main occupation in the area until the 1930s when five acres of land collapsed into an underground reservoir of brine.

The quiet village attracted L.S.Lowry to paint some of his 'Matchstick' masterpieces. Its other claim to fame is the famous Knott End to Fleetwood ferry that opened in 1894, although there's been a ferry service of sorts since before records began. Originally passengers would be transported by local fishermen but that duty now belongs to the Wyre Marine service.

It was at the cafe near the terminus that my story begins. My mother and I arrive to an almost empty eating establishment and take our seats near the window so that we can watch the world go by – well not quite the world! We order our meal and have a cuppa beforehand. It's quite important, at this juncture to explain that my mother is, at this time, in her mid 70's whilst I am still in my late 20's. The waitress is passing the time of day with us, when a commotion at the entrance sees a coach load of pensioners entering the restaurant.

They push and jostle their way to the best seats and it takes quite a while for things to calm down. Eventually order is restored and the cafe owner joins the waitress to see to everyone's order.

"I think I'll have fish and chips!"

"Well you'll not get better; Fleetwood's only over there!"

"I might try a pie."

"Batter doesn't agree with me, I think I'll stick to a piece of gammon!"

And so it goes on until I hear a slight muttering and an attempt at a whisper. If you're deaf, it's hard to whisper!

"That bloke over there looks like one of them Houghton Weavers!"

"Which one? Oh, that one over there. Hey you know, it might just be him."

"No it's not. Not tall enough!"

"He's sat down! How can you tell how tall he is!"

"It's definitely him!"

"Is it bloody hell, nothing like him at all!"

"I'll bet you it is!"

My mother and I have a little giggle to ourselves and continue with our meal. When we've finished I suggest we might try a sweet, "Unless you fancy an ice cream on the front?"

"Let's have another cuppa, then we can get the bill and have an ice cream outside."

"OK, I'll just go and spend a penny before we go. You order the teas."

So I get up from my seat and disappear into the lavatory. Yes. I washed my hands!

On returning to my chair, I see that my mother is in fits of laughter.

"What's tickled you?"

"You'll never guess what that bloke over there said when you were in the toilet."

"What? It must have been funny."

"When you went in the toilet, he came over and sat in your chair. Then he said, 'I don't want to be funny love, but is your husband one of the Houghton Weavers?'"

"Husband? Thanks a lot!"

I didn't know whether it was a compliment to my mother or an insult to me but we managed to laugh all the way to Pilling! We still do gigs at Pilling Memorial Hall. It's our longest ever continual gig; we've gone annually for well over thirty years and we are always treated royally by Eileen Bee, her granddaughters and the committee.

Queen's Lancashire Regiment

Following one of the recordings of the television show, we were relaxing in the Green Room, when our Stage Manager, Peter, introduces us to a very well spoken bloke. "Can I introduce you lads, this is Dickie, my new father-in-law. Dickie is the Colonel of the Queen's Lancashire Regiment based in Preston."

"Retired Colonel! Lovely to meet you gentlemen. You'll have to come and sing to our boys. We're over in Cyprus at the moment."

"That sounds great! We'd love to come; just give us a ring and we'll arrange something."

Great! A week in the sun in Cyprus will do us all good! We've never sung for the army before, it could be great for everybody concerned.

"Nice meeting you Dickie! We'll be in touch."

We were to find out later that Dickie wasn't his first name but his second name was Bird, hence the nickname! The Queen's Lancashire Regiment came into being in 1970 when the Lancashire Regiment (Prince of Wales Volunteers) and the Loyal Regiment (North Lancashire) were amalgamated. There are few campaigns in the history of the British army in which some predecessor unit of the regiment didn't take part. During the time we had dealings with the regiment they were involved in the Falklands aftermath, Bosnia, Iraq and also stationed in Cyprus. So Dickie rang us a few weeks later, "We'll sort out all the accommodation, food and transport. Are you still up for a visit with the lads?"

"Of course we are Dickie. Sounds like a great time for everyone. When do you want us to leave?"

"The weekend after next will be great! Also, I forgot to tell you but the lads are back from Cyprus."

"OK, but where do you want us to go?"

"The lads are in Northern Ireland at the moment."

"Where?"

"Bessbrook barracks in Armagh, Northern Ireland."

"That's not Cyprus, Dickie!"

"No, but they'll look after you like lords. You'll have a marvellous time!"

The village of Bessbrook was built as a 'model' village, like Bournville, Port Sunlight and Saltaire. It was built for the workers in the linen industry and on the premise of the three 'p's', in other words, there would be no public houses, no pawn brokers and, because it would be a model village there would be no need for police. There are still no pubs or pawn brokers in the village but the police presence was inevitable during 'the troubles'. The village took its name from the founder's wife, Elizabeth or 'Bess' Nicholson with the brook coming from a river running through the town.

The village, which has a cross religious representation in the town saw some of the worst violence during this time and the linen mill became headquarters to the British Army. A helicopter landing pad was established to supply other military outposts in the area and became the busiest helicopter pad in Europe. It wasn't to be until 2007 before the British presence withdrew from the area and closed their facilities in South Armagh.

But the troubles in Ireland did not start in the 1960s. Many hundreds of years before, the English and Irish had been at war. The problems go back to the 16th century, when a programme of colonisation by the English took place. The Roman Catholic aristocracy fled the Kingdom of Ireland to mainland Europe after several defeats in battle and the Protestant English and the Presbyterian Scottish made it their home. By the early 1700s there were reputed to be five Scottish and one English to every three Irishmen in the Province of Ulster.

By the end of the 18th Century steps were taken to end statutory discrimination against Catholics, who were given the right to buy their land from the landowners. In 1912 Ireland was given the right to rule itself as part of the United Kingdom of Great Britain and Ireland. Many people in England were against 'Home Rule' and tried to veto all progress. Unionists, the Irish who favoured a 'union' with Britain, were in a minority on the island but in the Province of Ulster, which was the counties of Antrim, Down, Armagh, Derry, Fermanagh and Tyrone, they were the majority. The English decided to divide the country into North, being the Province of Ulster and the South, which was the other 26 counties. These were both to lie under the jurisdiction of the United Kingdom but both parties were not happy with this. Great Britain granted the island independence in 1922 and it became 'The Irish Free state' but the Province of Ulster was given one month to either accept or opt out of the treaty. They chose to opt out and stay with Britain, which they did. The Irish Free State became the country of Eire or the Republic of Ireland in 1937. And that's it in a nutshell! But don't take my word for it; it's rather more complicated than that!

On the Road

During these early days we were, and still are, doing a lot of mileage. There are lots of tales to relate about journeys throughout this country and abroad. Going through towns with wonderful names like Lower Peover, Barrick in Elmett to name but two; playing games to occupy our time, like finding a registration whose number is one, then two and so on. They've got to be in order and I think I eventually reached the mid fifties before I gave up the ghost. Making phrases with the three letters of a number plate and so on; the more ridiculous the better!

We originally bought an old 'Bedford' van that had belonged to the RAF. We should have known that they would have hammered the engine because we had nothing but trouble with it. It eventually blew up on the way to Pilling when the gear stick fell out of the bottom of the vehicle and we nearly did a pole vault with the drive shaft. We eventually got alternative transport and arrive at the venue around 10pm. (We were due to start at 7.30pm.) Instead of shouting at us, the organisers took us into the back room and gave us supper before we started!

Once, on the way to Kendal, we had an amazing journey where we had three punctures! The first one was OK as we had a spare. We changed that and the spare got a flat. We drove to a service station on the flat tyre and had them both repaired but when we returned to the motorway we had a flat in another tyre. On each occasion we rang the venue to tell them what was going on and where we were but eventually I think they decided that we were making up the whole story. We still got to the gig and did our spot around two hours late!

Flat tyres, floods, blizzards or anything else for that matter could not deter the intrepid Weavers, as we made our way around our green and pleasant land.

We had a gig in Llandrindod Wells in Mid Wales; the journey took us through beautiful Welsh countryside with winding roads that swept up, down and round this dramatically stunning landscape. On arrival at the top of a hill we reach a set of traffic lights that had a sign below the lights which read "Possible three minute delay" with absolutely no reason for the delay; so we made one up! Above that small sign we attached a piece of card which read "Egg boiling Eisteddfod!"

We've had several vehicles over the years and all have stories to tell. We were once asked to join a Carnival parade and asked if we could go in our own vehicle which displayed the group name on its side. It was a Fiat and had a sliding side door which we left open to greet the public. Well, we left it open until it fell off! We drove all the way home from Leyland with the door in the boot and ourselves in the fresh air!

We were zooming up the motorway one evening when a police patrol car stopped us. The officer approached our vehicle and asked for the window to be wound down and spoke, "Good evening Wing Commander, having trouble taking off!"

"Sorry officer,"came our reply, "but we didn't realise we were travelling so fast!"

"I'm afraid I'm going to have to ask you to blow in this bag."

"Why, are your chips too hot!"

"Oh, we have a comedian! Please step out of the vehicle and come to my car sir."

On arrival in the back seat he continued, "Now sir, if you'd blow into this bag."

"I'm sorry constable but I can't do that!"

"Why not sir?"

"Because I have a card!" I produce the card and hand it over to the officer. The card reads 'This man is asthmatic and cannot blow into things!'

"That's perfectly understandable sir. However, I'm going to have to ask to come with me to the station so that we can take a blood sample!"

"I'm sorry officer but I can't do that!"

He's by now, getting rather exasperated, "Why not sir?"

"Because I've got a card!" The card reads, 'This man is anaemic and must not give blood!"

"I fully understand your predicament sir, but I'm afraid you'll need to accompany me to the station to give a urine sample!"

"I can't do that!"

"Why on earth not?" I produce the final card which reads 'This man is a Bolton Wanderers fan and mustn't have the pee taken out of him!'

Burnden Park

Burnden Park was the home of Bolton Wanderers from 1895 to 1997. The famous old ground had its fair share of triumph and tragedy. The club was formed in 1874 as Christ Church FC but following a few disagreements, it parted company with the church and became Bolton Wanderers FC in 1877. It was one of the original twelve members of the Football League which formed in 1888. In 1894 shares were raised to build a ground and, with the £4,000 that was raised Burnden Park was completed in August 1895. The capacity was 70,000 but numbers were dramatically reduced in the stadiums final two decades.

The FA cup final replay of 1901 took place at Burnden Park when Tottenham Hotspur beat Stoke City 3-1. The stadium was used as a backdrop to several feature films including 'A Kind of Loving' starring Alan Bates in 1962 and 'The Love Match' featuring Arthur Askey a decade earlier. It was the subject of an LS Lowry painting 'Going to the Match' which was purchased by the Professional Footballers association at Sotheby's auction rooms for £1,926,500.00 in 1999 and was a record price for a modern British painting.

In 1946 the biggest tragedy in British footballing history at the time, took place at the ground, when 33 people were crushed to death and over 400 were injured. It took place during an FA cup quarter final between Bolton and Stoke City. The crowd capacity had been exceeded by 15,000 and the official report recommended more rigorous control of ground sizes. We never learn do we?

By the late 1990s the ground was past its sell by date and it was decided to move to new premises. Part of the ground had been sold to pay debts and it was no longer capable of holding top flight games. So the decision was made to leave Manchester Road and move to a brand new stadium that was to be built in Horwich. In April 1997 Bolton Wanderers were already Division One Champions, when the final match took place at this fine old ground. The Houghton Weavers were known to be big fans of the club and were asked to join in the celebrations by leading the Community Singing before the match began.

It couldn't have been a greater honour to lead the singing at Wembley! I was quite emotional with everything that was going on. All the famous names from the past were in attendance and we had a fabulous time. The icing was put on the cake when John McGinlay scored the final goal as Bolton beat Charlton Athletic 4-1 after coming back from a goal down.

Many fans refused to make the journey to the new stadium which was named the 'Reebok' but eventually agreed that this was the future and the club had to move with the times. I spent many a happy afternoon at Burnden Park and have spent equally memorable afternoons and some evenings at our new home. Who would have guessed in the mid seventies, when Bolton were languishing in the fourth division of English football, that three decades later they would be sporting World Cup winning players in their team and playing against the cream of English football......we also play Manchester United as well!

Foo Foo's Palace

After many of our television recordings we'd have a few hours in Manchester to relax after a show. Just around the corner from Oxford Road studios was a night club called 'Foo Foo's Palace', run and owned by Frank 'Foo Foo' Lamarr, the biggest drag queen in the North of England. He chose Lamarr after Heddy Lamarr although his real name was Pearson. We'd call in and have a chat with Frank and his mother who was the 'doorman'! She'd collect money at the door whilst Foo Foo did his act. I don't think I've ever seen anybody in show business work as hard as him. When people arrived Foo Foo would be serving drinks behind the bar in a beautiful sequinned dress. As the place started to fill up, Frank would disappear, only to reappear on stage in another dress, to introduce everyone to the evening's entertainment. He would sing a few songs and tell quite smutty jokes to a packed audience of women who were on 'hen nights'. The audience was always ninety per cent female, hence our many visits! Well, you didn't think we went just to see Foo Foo did you?

During the evening he would appear on stage for three 'spots' as Foo Foo and at the end of the night he would appear as himself to end the evening entertainment. The place was always packed to the rafters and everybody loved his humour. He involved the audience throughout and invited the forthcoming 'brides' on stage and unmercifully took the micky with his highlight of the evening, the dance of the 'ruptured cucumber'.

Frank grew up in Ancoats, the son of a rag and bone man and left school with no qualifications. Although he worked as a drag queen in the local pubs and clubs, he was a handy boxer, so could take care of himself. He eventually raised enough money to buy the Picador club, followed by the Celebrity club which had a name change and became his famous 'Palace' and together with his beloved mother raised many hundreds of thousands of pounds for charity. With his mother Leah, whom he adored, he went shopping and had tea with her daily in the bungalow in Moston that he bought for her. They never discussed his sexuality, although Frank used to talk about being a young man in Ancoats and not knowing whether he was Arthur or Martha!

I once saw him play the lead part of Frank N Furter in the stage show of 'The Rocky Horror Show' at the Palace theatre and he was fabulous. He always said that if 'Frank' could pay his wages then he wouldn't have to rely on 'Foo Foo' but that was never the case and everyone who saw and loved him were quite happy about that.

So here we are going to nightclubs and finishing off in Chinatown for a meal! A far cry from a pint in the Red Lion and fish and chips on the way home! So that's showbiz!

Germany

We get a call from Brian, our manager. "How are you boys? Fancy a trip to Germany?"

"We certainly do. Where?"

"Well I've just had a phone call from the NAAFI asking if we could do a short tour of the Junior Ranks Clubs."

"Oh, I was expecting a gig with the Berlin Philharmonic but I suppose the Junior Ranks will suffice! What's the itinerary and when do they want us to go?"

"In about three weeks but they'll have a briefing when you arrive to sort out the exact timings and venues. I tried to get the sergeants and officers messes but they'd only do the 'squaddies' first time." The 'squaddies' being the junior ranks in the army.

"Do they want a folk group? I would have thought that a couple of exotic dancers would be more to their liking?"

"Don't worry lads it's going to be great. I don't think I'll be able to come with you though. I've quite a lot of work on at the moment."

"That sounds ominous! Never mind, it's a change from Lancashire and it should be fun!"

So preparations are made for our tour of Germany. There were lots of bases in Germany at the time and all entertainment was organised through the NAAFI. The Navy, Army and Air Force Institutes was a government organisation that was founded in 1921. They supply shops, clubs and recreation facilities on bases throughout the world and run bars, shops, supermarkets, laundrettes and cafes on the sites. They also run Royal Naval ships canteens. Commissioned officers are not supposed to use these facilities as they are seen as an intrusion into junior ranks private lives. All people who work for the NAAFI are civilians even though they wear naval uniforms. During World War II it had 7,000 canteens and over 100,000 personnel. It also controlled ENSA, the Entertainments National Service Association. And that's where we come in!

So we were following in the steps of such greats as Gracie Fields, George Formby and Vera Lynn or was it 'Dad's Army' or 'It Aint Half Hot Mum!' Accordingly, with a 'fine pair of shoulders' Sergeant Major 'Shut Up' Williams, Gunner 'Gloria' Beaumont, Private 'Stupid Boy' Pike and Lance Corporal 'Don't Panic!' Jones, embark on a voyage of discovery to the junior ranks clubs of Germany.

We travel to Hull to take the overnight ferry to Zeebrugge in the Netherlands. We can relax and have a good time on this trip. It's not like singing in 'bandit country' in South Armagh. Everyone's going to be pleasant and we'll absolutely wow the soldiers with our wit and repartee. Well that's what we keep telling ourselves on the journey via the North Sea to Europe. We stay up most of the night as the ferry has a disco and late bar. We thought we'd refrain from singing; there'll be enough of that in the next two weeks. We've been told that we should be working every night during our stay so it's going to be rather hectic.

During trips like these we would take our own sound equipment rather than hire Public Announcement (P.A.). For a while now we had a new recruit to our ranks by the name of Phil. He did everything from sorting out the merchandise, ordering drinks, arranging and mixing the sound, to wiping our noses! A jovial character with always a story to tell, Phil became a sixth Weaver, if Alan Fawkes was the fifth!

So Phil was driving the van through Europe without satellite navigation, mobile phone, ipad, or any of the new fangled stuff that is so freely available today. Although he's a great driver and everybody feels entirely safe in his company he invariably gets lost occasionally. There's nobody to ask as none of us speak German but we always get where we need to go. Our destination is the first German base somewhere in deepest Westphalia. We depart the ferry in Zeebrugge and make our way through the Netherlands passing 'A Bridge Too

Far' at Arnhem. This is the title of a very famous World War II film about September, 1944, when thousands of paratroopers fell from the sky, a hundred miles behind enemy lines, to secure several bridges across rivers in the Netherlands, so that the Allies could advance and cut off the German retreat. It was hoped that 'Operation Market Garden' if successful, would end the war by Christmas of that year. Unfortunately, the Germans regrouped and the troops from the British Isles and Poland were eventually evacuated after ten days of intense fighting, without securing the bridgehead.

We eventually arrive at our first destination which is a canteen on a huge army base in the middle of nowhere. We arrive at the gates and are greeted by several armed guards who want to know if we are here to blow up the base! When they realise we are the entertainment and there are no females with us they lose all interest. We are directed around the base and arrive at the venue where we will be performing; the canteen! It looks like any other canteen in a big factory of the period; large, bare walls, plastic chairs and tiled floor, totally unappealing and with no atmosphere whatsoever. There's nobody around, so we set up all the gear and hope we've put it in the right place and not used up too much space for the hundreds we hope will attend our first foray into Germany.

Once set up we need to eat! Asking around, it appears that the only place to get some sustenance is a 'schnell imbass' or 'fast food' establishment. They are all over the place but I would have preferred to sit down in a restaurant to eat. I've got a good appetite and a small roadside cafe doesn't appear to be the place to get a hearty meal. So when we go in, I order two meals because I probably won't get anything else today. When the meals arrive, it suddenly hits me that we are in Germany and they eat more than the Yanks! Two huge plates of Schnitzel and chips are placed in front of me. There's enough food for all five of us! I'm completely over-faced and manage to eat a few mouthfuls from one of the huge platters. Then we get into some conversation.

"So what do you think about this lot?"

"It should be OK. There are lots of people on the base so we should get a decent crowd."

"What if we don't?"

148

"We're getting paid aren't we? You'll just have to grin and bear it."

"I'm worried about the fact that we aren't of the female persuasion – apart from Phil."

"Speak for yourself ducky! I'll join you on stage if you like?"

"No, to be serious, all they are after is a disco and some boobs to look at!"

"They aren't all like David! There could be some folk enthusiasts."

"Let's not jump to conclusions. It could be a fabulous night. If it's not, there's always tomorrow."

So with a great deal of scepticism we return to the base where we are greeted by an officer of some sort.

"Houghton Weavers?"

"Yes, that's us!"

"My name is Captain John Spencer and I'll be your co-ordinator for the trip. Have you been to Germany before?"

"No, sir!"

"Call me John."

"No, John we've never been here before and we are feeling quite apprehensive."

"There's nothing to worry about lads. Just give 'em something to dance to and they'll be fine."

"But you can't dance to anything that we do!"

"Well you'd better start panicking now! Only joking! You'll be fine. Do what you normally do and, once they've had a few beers everything will be fine. If you get a few beers down it will be even less of a hassle."

"You're making us feel much better, John! What time do you want to start and when do you envisage the end?"

"Once there's a crowd in you can start. From then on in, it's up to you. We generally finish around midnight to give the lads a chance to have a fight before they go to bed!"

I don't think he's joking! It's going to be horrendous!

"The bar's over here, I'll probably have gone before you finish but here's my phone number should you need any help or advice. Good luck!"

And he was gone!

149

We sit around morbidly contemplating our fate until one or two squaddies begin to arrive; and I mean one or two! By the time we get to around 8.30pm there's probably less than twenty in a canteen that could probably hold a thousand or more! The barman introduces himself and tells us that it probably won't get more populated until around ten o'clock.

"You might as well start. You're a folk group aren't you?"

"Yes!"

"They don't like folk around here so you might as well get it over with."

God help us, here we go!

So we climb onto a recently constructed stage made from beer crates and eight by four plywood. We are sliding around, trying to keep our balance and go through our whole repertoire. Fast songs, slow songs, ballads, funny songs (well we think they are!), monologues, jokes and our audience of young blokes in their late teens drink Grolsch beer and talk amongst themselves. I can remember audiences like this from the social clubs back home but for the rest of the lads it is an unknown phenomenon that they just can't cope with.

Things are going amazingly badly when a new audience member joins his mates and Norman thinks he'll try a joke – bad mistake! The guy's got a striped shirt on and Norman wittily jokes, "Fancy coming out in your pyjama coat!" His mates think it's extremely funny, or is it that they realise what's going to happen next. The young guy slowly gets to his feet, beer in hand and saunters towards the stage. He climbs onto the palettes and walks slowly towards Norman, who by this time had become a much whiter shade than the nicotine stained walls. He slowly grabs Norman by his shirt and lifts him about four inches from the floor. Norman is trying to tip toe around the stage whilst looking hopelessly at the rest of us for support.

Quietly the young man whispers into Norman's ear, "Say something like that again and I'll shove this bottle of beer where the sun doesn't shine. That is if it will fit in next to that guitar!"

"Sorry mate! Only a joke!"

"Well I didn't think it was funny. My girlfriend bought me this shirt and I'll not be able to wear it again because of you."

"Of course you will, it's a lovely shirt!"

"Oh, no he won't!" comes a chorus from the six or seven of his mates who are baying for blood!

"I think we'll do one more song and the take a break. Hope you're all enjoying yourselves?"

"When do the dancers come on?" echoes one smart Alec from the rear of the room.

Ignore him! Ignore him! "Just introduce the song Norman and let's get off!"

So we end the first of what was to be more than a dozen shows in places like this with audiences like this and think, *What have we let ourselves in for?*

We take a short break without speaking to each other, each wrapped up in the thoughts of what will happen in the next two weeks. The second half, of around forty-five minutes, seems to last in the region of five hours. We end the show and walk off the stage to the sound of our own footsteps.

"Pack the gear and let's get out of here. Everybody help Phil and we'll be out of here in about twenty minutes!"

"I'm having a drink or two before I go home!"

"So am I!" Norman says, "Phil, if you want a drink I'll drive back to the digs!"

"Are you sure?"

"Yeah, no problem, you look like you need a drink!"

"So do you but you don't partake!"

Several pints and jokes later we have relaxed and feel ready for the journey home. We ride home solemnly, all with our own thoughts as to how the next few days are going to pan out. It just might be a blip; things might get substantially better. After a couple of drinks everything always feels better.

"Phil, this doesn't look like the same road we came down earlier."

"No, you'll probably be better getting back on the motorway. There's a sign post ahead." He manages to get back on the autobahn and appears to go in the right direction. After a couple of miles he leaves the motorway and realises within a couple of minutes that he's taken the wrong turning again. Everyone is now beginning to take notice of the direction we are taking. He turns round and gets back on the motorway. At the next junction he signals to leave the road and everyone screams that this isn't the right turning.

"But it's the junction we came off earlier."

"Is it bloody hell! We need to go another twenty miles before we come off!"

"But the signpost is the same one as before. That's the sign for our town."

"What is?"

"There, it says 'Ausfahrt'; that's where we are staying."

"You stupid idiot! 'Ausfahrt' means 'exit', it's on every one of the bloody signs!"

Following our brief German language lesson we eventually arrive home and immediately bed down for the night with the hope that things will improve in the morning.

The accommodation where we were staying was fairly central for all of the first seven dates and then we'd change the hotel for the following week. We'd decided that the most prudent way to organise the day was to drive to the barracks following breakfast, set up the gear for the evening and if we'd enough time we could explore the local vicinity. First things first, we approach the motorway and explain to Norman that 'Einfahrt' isn't the nearest town along the autobahn but a sign that says, 'Entrance', although, following last night's escapade, Phil has decided he won't drink again for the duration of our stay!

We arrive at another huge barracks and find our way to a small social club with stage, curtains and a completely different atmosphere to the previous night. The steward is a guy from Liverpool and explains how things work on these trips.

"You'll get the occasional canteen but most of the venues are small social clubs and the atmosphere is much better. You'll be fine lads! The places you want to beware of are such a place and such a place. Last night were children but the animals live at these places!"

We look at our itinerary and find that in the next few nights we'll be visiting all of those places that he mentioned.

"Don't worry boys", I explain, "once we get used to it we'll be fine! Let's just enjoy ourselves."

Phil sets up his sound equipment at the back of the room whilst we organise everything on stage. We have a small changing room that is more than adequate for our needs so things are looking up! They are expecting a better crowd than last night as it's Friday and the squaddies tend to go out more when the weekend is approaching. As it gets to stage time the place is filling up and there appears to be a friendly atmosphere in the auditorium.

We go on stage at approximately eight o'clock and the first couple of songs appear to be going down alright I decide I will try a ballad so Norman introduces "When you were Sweet Sixteen". I begin the song when I see a member of the staff walking out from behind the bar. He is pulling what I now know to be wheelie bin, although I'd never seen one before. As he walks around the room he lifts the lid and proceeds to drop empty bottles into the receptacle. This make quite a loud sound but it is nothing compared to what is about to happen! As he approaches the squaddies tables they decide to give him a hand, by standing on the chairs and throwing the empty beer bottles into the said wheelie bin. If I thought that the barman was making a noise then I was to be rudely awakened by the ensuing 'explosions' made by the bottles hitting other bottles at high speed and disintegrating into a million pieces.

Don't worry Tony. Keep calm! The song's nearly finished and they've been OK up to this moment. I'll not try another ballad this evening. In fact I might put a dress on and do my version of 'the time warp'!

The song mercifully reaches its conclusion and it appears things are getting back to normal when a huge bloke at the back of the room stands up and shouts, "Sing the Wild Rover!"

"No problem pal, we'll do that in a while."

"No, you'll do it now if you know what's good for ye!"

"Don't listen to him!" pipes up another young bloke on the front row,

"Sing a song from Liverpool. Bugger that Scottish git!"

"What about a Geordie song?"

"Maybe later."

"Maybe now!"

Next thing we know, the Scottish guy at the back of the room climbs up onto the table and, with feet and arms swinging, dives towards the Liverpudlian. The Geordie decides to join the fray and flies across the room to trade punches with a Welshman and the Cockney gives the Brummie a black eye. We decide to leg it off stage whilst Phil puts the lid on the sound desk and joins us in the changing room. All hell is let loose in the hall and we sit cringing in our little hidey-hole whilst the building echoes to the sound of breaking glasses, tables and noses!

Eventually things appear to calm down and an official looking gentleman appears in our cubicle. "Sorry about the trouble gentlemen! My name's Lieutenant Jones and the MP's have got them all out on the square!"

"What does that mean, is the night over?"

"I'm afraid it is for this evening gentlemen but don't worry you're here for a few more nights yet!"

"What's going to happen to that lot?"

"Oh, don't worry, there're finishing the fight off on the parade ground, then they'll all be on a charge tomorrow morning."

"You're letting them finish the fight?"

"Oh, yes! They are soldiers and we don't want to knock their fighting spirit. I know what you're thinking; might it happen again. The answer to that is, probably, so we'll put MP's on the stage for the rest of your shows. Don't worry boys; you'll come to no harm. You've got the British Army to protect you!"

"Gents, I think it's time we had a meeting!"

"Meeting!" we all cry in unison. From the group's inception, it was always protocol, when we hit a hurdle or a problem, to call a meeting. At the end of the discussion there would be a fully democratic vote to agree whatever Norman decided!

"Well, what do you think guys?"

"It's not working is it?"

"No, it's a bloody disaster and I think we should call it a day!"

"What, do you mean, go home?"

"That's exactly what I mean!"

"But what about the money?"

154

"The money might be good for some groups but it isn't brilliant."

"Can we do without it?"

"Money's always useful but do we need it that badly?"

"Well as far as I'm concerned, I think we should go back to the hotel, pack up all our gear and drive to Zeebrugge for the ferry."

"Well I agree with Norman but will there be a backlash?"

"I'm sure they won't book us again but is anybody bothered about that?"

"Not me!"

"Me neither! What do you think, Tony?"

"I agree with everyone. It's been a total disaster. The squaddies aren't bothered about listening to us, they want dancing dolly birds to ogle at!"

"What about John, the boss man?"

"My idea would be to drive to the ferry port and phone him when it's too late to do anything else!"

"Well, David, what do you think?"

"I agree with everyone but I'd like to add a little personal plea."

"What on earth is that?"

"Well, I agree that we leave right away and get out of Germany but could I ask that to add a bit of enjoyment we stay for a night in Amsterdam?"

"We'll not ask why but I agree; all in favour?"

"Aye!"

"Motion carried, as John Wayne would say; let's get the hell out of here!"

So we were on our way home via Amsterdam.

Bad Nights

Listening to this story you might be led to believe that life on the road goes from one bad night to another. You couldn't be further from the truth but the bad nights are the ones you remember more than most. For example, we often relate a story about an evening we spent at 'Quaffers', a night club near Stockport. It was a private affair for a large local firm of draughtsmen and women. We were to be the entertainment for around one thousand members of the firm plus relatives and friends.

The nightclub, 'Quaffers', originally 'The Warren' was owned by a Manchester legend with a murky past. Dougie Flood was a member of 'The Quality Street' gang who, it is alleged, ran organised crime in and around Manchester for many years, although others believed them to be no more than a group of friends who had a criminal past. There's an urban myth (I wish it were true) that Dougie, some of his gangster buddies and several police, turned back the Kray twins at Manchester's Piccadilly Station, when they arrived to try and establish a northern arm to their criminal empire. The Quality Street gang were the subject of the Thin Lizzie hit, 'The Boys are back in Town'.

With such a shady background, it's quite amusing to find that Dougie Flood refused entry to his club, to men with shaven heads, tattoos and earrings saying that they gave his club a bad image and argued that these fashions were associated with the drugs culture. He wished to maintain higher standards for his clientele!

We arrive at the club this particular evening and bosses from our employers start laying down the law.

"First of all gentlemen, we'll be doing a short sketch which you will play the music for!"

"What music?"

"It's scripted here!"

"But only Alan can read music!"

"Well you'll need to sort it out quickly".

"I'm sorry but it isn't that easy. Can you read music?"

"No, but it can't be that difficult! We need to do the sketch to impress our bosses."

"Well, you'll impress your bosses even more without music. They'll think we've done all the work if you have music".

"Maybe you're right! We'll scrap the music then!"

Thank God for that! It would have been a complete disaster.

"OK, we'll go ahead with our sketch around nine o'clock and then we'll introduce you lot!"

"How long do you want us to do?"

"No more than forty minutes, I don't think they could take much more than that!"

"Thanks a lot!"

So these obnoxious three blokes leave us alone in the changing room and we are left to plan what we'll do.

"Did you see that manuscript he pulled out? There's not a cat in hell's chance of us playing that!"

"Don't worry; we're not doing it now so let's concentrate on the show. There are around a thousand people out there. There will be loads of other firms represented here, so if it goes down well, we'll get loads of work!"

"I think the Three Musketeers are returning so let's make ourselves scarce!"

Sure enough, the guys arrive back and take to the stage with a continuous stream of 'in' jokes that mean nothing to anybody, apart from the bosses in the top office. Meanwhile we are honing our act backstage in the hopes of completely wowing them all. Eventually, the torture comes to an end and the Three Stooges make their way backstage whilst patting each other admiringly on the backs.

Then it arrives! The MD takes to the stage and thanks the Three Wise Men and comes to the best introduction we've never had!

"Ladies and gentlemen, now it's time to introduce the stars of this evening, direct from BBC television, the fabulous Houghton Weavers AND dinner is served!"

So, as we begin to climb the steps to the stage, one thousand people get up from their seats and make their way to the dining room, where dinner is being served! We arrive on stage to be greeted by the backs of 980 people and the fronts of just over a dozen who had stayed for the show! We thank these few for remaining in their seats to watch the show.

"Oh, we're just waiting for the queue to die down then we'll be following them!"

From that point onwards we added a clause to our contracts that read, 'no food to be served whilst the group are on stage'. A bit too late for that particular evening!

Free Trade Hall

The Free Trade Hall in Manchester was an amazing venue. Originally built, by public subscription, between the years of 1853 and 1856, on St.Peter's Field, the site of the 'Peterloo Massacre'. A red plaque adorns the side of the building; it reads: "St. Peter's Fields, The Peterloo Massacre. On the 16th August 1819 a peaceful rally of 60,000 pro-democracy reformers, men, women and children, was attacked by armed cavalry resulting in 15 deaths and over 600 injured."

The building was built to celebrate the repeal of the Corn Laws; laws designed to protect the price of home grown cereal from competition from less expensive foreign imports. The problem was that the factory workers wages were low and food prices were high so the only people to suffer, as usual, were the ones at the bottom of the pile. Protests took place until eventually the law was repealed in 1846, making a significant increase in 'free trade', hence the name of the building.

The Free Trade Hall was home of the world famous Hallé Orchestra from 1857 to 1996. The pianist Charles Hallé, a founder member of the Liverpool Philharmonic Orchestra set up an orchestra to perform for the 'Art Treasures Exhibition' in Manchester. He continued working with the orchestra, who gave its first formal concert on 30th January 1858. Over the years the institution has had its ups and downs, mainly financial, but still exists today in its new home at the majestic Bridgewater Hall.

The Free Trade Hall was bombed during the Manchester blitz and the interior was rebuilt between 1950-51 and opened as a concert hall in 1951 and that building is where my little story starts! The hall seated around 2,000 people, with around 1,200 on the balcony that swept from the stage, around the back of the hall, to the stage on the opposite side of the room. The balcony was quite wide and encroached over the front of the stage on both sides. We had appeared there a couple of times, to a sell out crowd and were really looking forward to this visit. Our sound guys had arrived at lunchtime and we checked the sound when we arrived.

It's show-time and we enter to see a full throng of people sitting in eager anticipation. We say our hello's and sing our first song. At the end of the number we notice that the crowd in the stalls greet us with unbridled enthusiasm whilst the crowd in the balcony applaud only lightly. Then we here a solitary voice from the rear of the circle. "We can't hear you!"

We ignore that particular plea as our sound guys will be sorting that problem out as we speak. Into the second song and we get a similar reaction except around a dozen cry, "Can't hear you!"

"We're sorry about this ladies and gentlemen. I promise this will be sorted out in the next couple of minutes!"

Third song ends and a cacophony of a hundred or two voices scream, "We can't hear you!"

"Ladies and gentlemen," we reply, "we've obviously got a slight problem here. We'll leave the stage for a few minutes but promise, when we return, everything will be back to normal!"

We walk off stage and scream, via the intercom, to our sound engineer to come back stage.

"What the bloody hell's going on? The ones in the balcony can't hear us. Sort out the problem quickly or we are in the doo doo!"

So for the next few minutes, our sound people are rushing backwards and forwards checking every eventuality, when one of them spots the problem.

"The speakers are underneath the balcony, so everyone downstairs can hear but the ones above can't!"

"Well, can it be sorted?..............in two minutes?"

An engineer from the Free Trade Hall saunters by and asks if all is well?

"Is it bloody hell! There are twelve hundred people in there that can't hear us!"

"Well you could always connect your sound equipment to the 'house PA' and we could amplify your sound throughout the hall; simple!"

"Can it be done right away?"

"Just needs two wires to connect us together; we'll have some in the engineers room.............two ticks!"

Two wires arrive and are joined to our gear; we walk back on stage and say, 'hello' and everyone in the balcony begins clapping as a means of telling us that they can hear.

Problem solved! If everything were that simple!

Because every room is different there will always be sound issues to deal with but this was a problem of our own making. It never happened again!

The Free Trade Hall has heard major speeches by Benjamin Disraeli and Winston Churchill, Kathleen Ferrier sang Elgar's 'Land of Hope and Glory' at the re-opening in 1951, the only time she sang that particular song in her whole career. Bob Dylan, Pink Floyd and the Sex Pistols have all trod these famous boards but did any of them have trouble with the sound? ....probably not!

City Varieties

My family was fortunate enough to get a television when I was about eleven or twelve years old. One of the shows that enthralled me more than any, was the long running, 'Good Old Days', hosted by the garrulous Leonard Sachs who enchanted me with his vocal dexterity. I sat spellbound watching Arthur Askey, Tessie O'Shea, Ken Dodd and roared with laughter to the one I thought was funniest of all, Sandy Powell. These legends were walking in the footsteps of Charlie Chaplin, Harry Houdini and Marie Lloyd. Who would think that many years later I would be treading those very same boards!

Would you believe that this Grade II listed building began life as the 'singing room' in the upstairs of a pub! The landlord developed it into a place of music hall and variety that continues to this day.......the last surviving music hall in Britain. It was built in 1865 as an extension to the White Swan public house by Charles Thornton and named "Thornton's New Music Hall and Fashionable Lounge". When Brian, our manager, rang to say that we'd got a booking at one of entertainment's most famous emporiums, I was ecstatic.

It was everything I'd dreamed of! The ceilings were too low, the rooms were too small and smoke filled, the corridors too narrow, the stairs too steep.....wonderful! We had to carry everything up the back stairs to the front of the stage, lift them some six feet in the air to access the rostrum and be careful not to see them roll back down because the 'rake' of the stage was excessive. Once on stage, we'd line up, the four of us, and realise the ones on the outside could shake hands with the people in the adjacent boxes. The audience were not polite like other theatres but felt it was their duty to join in the act. In other words, everything about the place screamed 'show business' and you know what, there's no business like it!

So here we were, doing missionary work in deepest Yorkshire! We'd worked a few times with that wonderful all round entertainer, Roy Castle, who hailed from Scholes, near Holmfirth, the home of 'Last of the Summer Wine'. Roy was the son of a railway worker and was a dancer and musician as a child. He moved to Cleveleys, near Blackpool, so that he could pursue a career as an entertainer. He turned professional in 1953 and worked as a stooge for Jimmy James and Jimmy Clitheroe and by 1958 had appeared on the Royal Variety Show for the first time. He had multiple television appearances to his credit including a part in the film, 'Carry on up the Khyber' but his biggest credit was probably as presenter of 'Record Breakers' for over twenty years. During his time on the show he personally broke nine world records. The two most interesting, as far as I am concerned, was playing the same tune on 43 different instruments and being the fastest tap dancer in the world. He tapped 1,440 times in a minute, which equates to 24 taps per second, in 1973.

When we worked with him, we would extol the virtues of the great county of Lancashire. In reply he would tell this story. "Many hundreds of years ago, the population of Britain all lived along the East Coast. Foraging parties would explore the hinterland and gradually work their way westwards. Eventually they would arrive at the barrier that we now call the Pennines. They would slowly make their way up this formidable range of hills until they reached the summit. On arrival there they were met with a huge sign that said, simply, 'Lancashire'. At that point the ones that could read turned back!"

What a load of rubbish!

Home with mummy!

All my mates called me a 'mummy's boy' because I stayed at home until I was thirty two! They can say what they like! I know which side my bread's buttered! We had a great relationship; I paid the bills and she made our house a home for any one of my friends who would appear on our doorstep at a minute's notice. They weren't calling me 'mummy's boy' when they were eating the meals she'd prepared or washing and ironing their shirts. I used to stay out till very early in the morning and I would be arriving home when she was getting up. We very rarely had rows and I think she enjoyed the company of my many friends.

She would regularly awaken on a weekend morning to find bodies strewn around the house. Rather than cause a commotion, she'd attend to whatever she was doing and work around the carcasses, making brews for any that woke up. Eventually life would begin to flow into these corpses and everyone would help to bring the house back to normal. Finally, breakfast was served, when I'd been to the shop for an extra loaf, some bacon, sausage and eggs. She became friends with all of the visitors and received birthday and Christmas cards from many of them for years to come.

Many years later when 'Amy' was ninety we had a big party in her honour. She was, by this time, living in sheltered accommodation in Westhoughton. All the family would visit regularly and she was never short of company. The accommodation had a communal lounge where anyone could entertain friends, residents and family, so it was decided that the party would take place there. When dates were sorted out as to when the celebration would occur, it was plainly obvious that I would be working. It wasn't too much of a problem, as I visited her regularly and would hear all about the festivities from neighbours, friends and family.

As a treat, I decided to buy her a grey Amazonian parrot. It was very expensive (£500) but could speak several languages which I thought she might find entertaining when her friends visited. As I couldn't attend the get together, I had the bird delivered by special courier, the day before her party.

A couple of days after the party I went round to see how everything went.

"Hiya mother, did you have a nice birthday party?"

"Oh, it was lovely; singing, dancing, great buffet, we had a wonderful time."

"What did you think about that present I had sent round for you?"

"Great! The meat just fell off the bone!"

"What, you didn't eat it did you?"

"Yes, it was delicious!"

"But it cost me five hundred pounds, it could speak seven languages!!"

"Well, it should have said something, shouldn't it?"

Sparks

SPARKS is a medical research charity dedicated to funding research into a range of conditions that affect babies and children. Their aim is to diagnose, treat and improve the quality of life for babies and young children. It was founded in 1960 when leading sports personalities of the day were recruited by Duncan Guthrie to raise money within their sport for this charity. Princess Michael of Kent is their royal patron and many famous personalities, both sporting and otherwise are involved with their tremendous work.

We'd been asked to play in a 'Sparks' golf tournament on the Isle of Man. Now, although I don't play golf I'd been roped in because the Weavers were part of the evenings' entertainment, after the round had finished. There's a reason I don't play golf and I'll try to explain. I know that lots of people say golf is a game that ruins a good walk but I love almost every sport. When people participate in the game they very quickly get 'hooked' and that is the very reason I steer clear! I don't mind getting totally involved with a game that lasts an hour or two but golf is all day of a job and I wouldn't be able to give it my full attention.

My friend, Paul, had invited us over to the island and a very close friend of his was in attendance. Paul Fletcher, 'Fletch', an ex – footballer and great wit, was helping to organise the day. The golf teams would consist of three people, who would pay a considerable amount of money to participate in a round. Once on the first tee, they would be joined by a celebrity for the rest of the day. Following the round of golf, all members of the team would be joined by partners for an evening meal, presentation of prizes and entertainment.

I'd been wandering the golf course during the day, watching all the famous people who had been participating in the event. After the golf, we would all shower and dress for dinner. A pre - dinner drink in the bar would be followed by grace given by Sir Norman Wisdom, who lived on the island. I'd not heard that 'Fletch' had been up to his tricks which was unusual, until I heard a commotion around the kitchen area.

I went over to see what was going on and a young waitress gave me the low down. "Do you know the gentleman over there, sir?" she asks, pointing to Fletch.

"Yes, he's a friend of mine. Any problems?"

"Well sir, apparently, the evening will conclude with an appearance of a donkey. It's the mascot of the charity and I'm in charge of it!"

"So?"

"Well it's tethered downstairs near the back door and Mr. Fletcher has asked me to collect all the bread rolls that have not been eaten. I then have to go downstairs and feed them to the donkey."

This is one of Fletch's tricks. He's up to no good!

"That's fine!"

"No it isn't!"

"Why?"

"Because I've collected all the bread rolls, gone downstairs to the kitchen to feed the donkey and it's not there!"

"Are you sure?"

"Of course I'm sure!"

"Have you looked around for it?"

"I don't have to look around. I know exactly where it should be. What am I going to say to Mr. Fletcher?"

"Show me!" I insist. So we go downstairs to the kitchen entrance where the donkey is supposed to be tied and find a long length of sisal role that had been neatly chewed at one end!

There was never a donkey here! It's one of Fletch's practical jokes. He's just tied a piece of rope to the drainpipe and frayed the other end!

"Don't worry, miss, I'll go and speak to Mr. Fletcher. You just go back to waiting on your table. I'll sort it out!"

So I go back upstairs and sure enough, Fletch is rolling around in fits of laughter.

"Sorry, Tony, but the poor girl was so serious!"

"I think you'd better go and apologise."

"Maybe later. I'll let her sweat a bit then give her a good tip before she goes home!"

Paul Fletcher played for Bolton Wanderers and Burnley and following retirement from football due to a knee injury, eventually became Chief Executive of Burnley football Club. He is now one of Europe's leading experts of stadia and was responsible for the Alfred McAlpine Stadium in Huddersfield, the Reebok stadium, Bolton and was invited by the FA to become commercial director of the new Wembley stadium. After 18 months he resigned his position to 'spend more time with his wife and family in the Lancashire sunshine!'

A female nurse tees off at the third hole but slices her ball and hits a man standing on the next green. He collapses with his hand between his legs. The nurse runs over and says, "Don't worry, I have medical training. I can help reduce the pain!"

She opens the man's' trousers and massages his privates. After a while she asks if he feels any better. He replies, "Yes thanks but I think you broke my thumb!"

Or the golfer who drives his new Honda car on to the forecourt of an attended garage. As the employee is filling his car with petrol he notices a couple of golf tees on the passenger seat.

"Excuse me sir, but what are those things on the passenger seat?"

"They are tees", replies the golfer.

"What are they for", comes the response.

"Well I put my balls on them when I'm driving!!"

"My God", retorts the assistant, "those Japanese think of everything!"

Granada

We'd been working for the BBC television and radio for a while now, so independent television took a fancy to us. We were invited to do several shows for Granada including one to celebrate their twenty-fifth year in Manchester. It was a similar type of programme to 'This is your Life' whereby couples, who were celebrating their silver weddings on the same week as the television company, were introduced to their celebrity and sporting heroes during the half hour show which talked about the highlights of their previous twenty-five years. Richard Madeley presented the show and the couple involved used to babysit me when I was a child. We chatted about my formative years and sang a song for them. Mr. and Mrs. Oakes were also big fans of Wigan rugby and nearly fell off their seats when the legendary Billy Boston made an appearance. William John Boston was born in Tiger Bay, Cardiff in 1934 and played for Pontypridd and Neath rugby union clubs. He was serving with the Royal Signals in Catterick when Wigan rugby league noticed his talents. He became a living legend and scored 478 tries for Wigan during his career. He also played 31 times for Great Britain and was elected to the Rugby league Hall of Fame, the Welsh Sports Hall of Fame and, together with Shaun Edwards, became the first member of Wigan's Hall of Fame. He was awarded the MBE in 1986 and the East Stand at the DW stadium in Wigan has borne his name since 2009. What a gentle giant he was!

Besides several slots on the Granada news programme, we were also invited to appear on their new Saturday morning show aimed at children. We had just issued a single during our time with EMI which would be launched on the early Saturday morning show titled, "The Fun Factory". It was set in one of the massive old mills that were adjacent to Granada studios at the time. There were several 'sets' in the huge building and we were to perform within an area divided by bails of straw.

All the cameramen were in fancy dress so that any cross shots would see a caveman, super hero or the like cavorting around the studio. There were hundreds of children creating complete havoc wherever they were placed in the mill. These would be herded from set to set so as to appear there were thousands rather than hundreds of kids in the venue. We had just released a single called, 'The Martians have landed in Wigan' and were there to publicise it. As part of the deal, EMI had two huge costumes made by the creators of 'It's a Knockout!" and we had a couple of mates prancing round the studios looking just as stupid as the cameramen and engineers.

Besides us, one of the guests this particular morning was the "Hee Bee Gee Bees", who parodied Bee Gees songs. The three members sang in very high pitched voices, holding hair dryers in front of their faces to keep their hair blowing backwards in a copycat version of one of the originals videos. They consisted of Philip Pope who later appeared in the radio version of 'Hitchhikers guide to the Galaxy', the comedy series 'Who Dares Wins' and as a character in 'Only Fools and Horses'. Michael Fenton Stevens became a cast member of the satirical, 'Spitting Image' TV show and finally the last member was Angus Deayton who was to star as the ill fated neighbour of Victor Meldrew in 'One Foot in the Grave' and the long running presenter of 'Have I got News for You'.

The Hee Bee Gee Bees released a single and two albums that did about as well as ours, which wasn't that well! They were backed in the studio by members of 10cc and Sad Café who did considerably better than both of us!

So here we are, getting ready to appear on live television in front of a massive national audience. We are ready, the cameras are ready and it's about two minutes before the red light goes on, when Denis shouts, "My bass isn't working!"

"Engineer!" cries the producer, "bass not working! Sort it out please, you got about two minutes!"

So an engineer, dressed as a tiger, scurries over to Denis and asks, "What's the problem, mate?"

"The bass cabinet is not working, listen!"

"I can't hear anything", replies the engineer.

"I know", screams Denis, "that's because it's not working!"

"No problem mate, just keep plucking the strings and I'll check the cabinet."

"One minute!", comes the voice from the floor manager.

"Still not working!"

"No! Hurry up!", cries Denis.

"Thirty seconds!"

Another engineer appears and they clamour round the cabinet.

"Ten seconds!"

"Nine!"

"Stand clear!" shouts Denis and gives the cabinet an almighty kick that moves it about a foot.

"Five, four, three!"

"It's Working!"

And off we go! Easy as pie!

We also appeared on a show called, 'The Video Entertainers', produced by Johnny Hamp. It was similar to the amazingly popular 'Comedians' using the same format. Acts would do a half hour set in the studio which would then be edited down to one song, followed by a comedian telling a couple of jokes, followed by a magician, followed by another song, etc. The problem was that the comedians would follow each other on stage. The canny ones would listen to all the others but those with more ego than intelligence would go on last and tell joke after joke that had already been told, to absolute silence from the audience. When it came to editing, the ones who hadn't listened were not included in the finished product.

This is Your Life

We were contacted and asked if we'd like to participate in an edition of the famous programme. It was hosted by Michael Aspel at the time and the recipient was to be Sister Aquinas, head teacher at St. Winifred's school in Stockport. She was retiring her headship and Granada thought they could do a programme about her life which ended up as a programme about her choir! They had released a single in 1980 which became that year's Christmas number one and knocked John Lennon off the top spot!. The song, 'There's No One Quite Like Grandma' spent two weeks at number one and a total of eleven weeks in the charts. The children had previously sung on another number one hit when they accompanied 'Brian and Michael' in 'Matchstalk Men and Matchstalk Cats and Dogs', which tells the story of L.S. Lowry. The producer and writer of 'Grandma' was Gordon Lorenz who wrote the song to tie in with the Queen Mother's 80th birthday. It was one of the last singles to sell over a million copies and EMI offered him a job. He was to become one of the most prolific producers in the music industry and recorded such diverse acts as Larry Adler, Shirley Bassey, Charlotte Church, Atomic Kitten and Cliff Richard!

Sister Aquinas was joined on stage by the choir, ourselves, who sang a song live on set, Brian and Michael and by video link to Abba in Sweden, as the choir had recently 'guested' on several of their shows. There were also relatives and friends who had travelled many miles to join in the celebration. So a fabulous night was had by all.

After the recording a buffet was served at a local hotel where everyone could say their 'hello's' and give their congratulation to a wonderful teacher and friend.

This reminds me of the nun who hails a cab. The driver seems fascinated with his new 'fare' to the point that the nun has to ask; "Excuse me my son, is there something bothering you?"

"Sorry sister, it's not often that I pick a nun up."

"Is that all that's bothering you?" asks the nun.

"Well sister, there is something else but I don't want to offend you in any way."

"My son, when you've been a nun as long as I've been, there's nothing anyone could say that I would find offensive."

"Well, sister, it's actually a request."

"And what's the request?"

"Well I hope you don't mind but I've always had a fantasy about kissing a nun."

"Unusual" replies the nun, "but let's see what we can do about it. There are a couple of 'musts'. Firstly, you must not be married and secondly you must be a Catholic!"

"Well, actually sister, I am single and I am a Catholic!"

"OK!" replies the nun, "pull up over into that alleyway".

She proceeds to give him a smacker on the lips that would make a call girl blush.

On resumption of the journey the cabbie starts to cry.

"Whatever is the matter my son?" she asks.

"Forgive me sister but I have sinned and lied. I'm not single but married and I'm actually a Jew!"

"Don't worry my son" replies the nun, "I'm called Kevin and I'm going to a fancy dress party!"

Ashes Cricket

I'd never been much of a participant of the game of cricket although I love to watch it. I have sat and watched every single ball bowled in a test match which, if you don't know, lasts at least seven hours a day, for 5 days. I've watched Lancashire at Old Trafford; that's the proper Old Trafford, not the pretend one, where they play football! I've seen England on quite a few occasions when a Test match has come to town. There are numerous things that Old Trafford is famous for; in 1956, Jim Laker took 19 wickets during a match, a feat that will almost certainly never be beaten. Much later, in 1993, Shane Warne bowled the 'ball of the century' when he took Mike Gatting's wicket. It is the second oldest Test venue and staged the first Ashes Test match in 1884 but the most notable event, I think, is that Manchester holds the record for the most days lost in a Test match, to the weather!

I decided to go on the third day of the Test in August 1981. The series was heading for a climax as England was poised to win an Ashes series when they had looked completely down and out. Ian Botham had been made captain of England the previous year but it had not been a happy time. He had lost form and the team was playing badly. After two Tests, England had lost one and drawn one. Botham scored two 'ducks' in the second match and memorably walked off the Lords pitch to complete silence from the MCC members. He was never to acknowledge them again when he played at Lords.

Following the game he was consequently sacked or resigned, depending on source, although Alec Bedsar, chairman of selectors, said he would have been fired in any event! The third Test didn't start any better and England was forced to 'follow on' after a disastrous start. At one point, in their second innings, they were 135 for the loss of seven wickets, when Ian Botham strode to the crease. He is reported to have said to his batting partner, Graham Dilley, "Right then, let's have a bit of fun!" He consequently scored 149 not out and gave the team a chance. Next day, Bob Willis took 8 wickets at the cost of only 43 runs and England won a match that, after two days, Ladbrokes had them at 500/1 outsiders. The odds were so ridiculous when there were only two teams that Rodney Marsh and Dennis Lillee, two of the Australian team, had a bet on England to win!" They won by the margin of 18 runs and it was the first time since1895 that a team, having been forced to follow on, had gone on to win the match. Man of the match – Ian Botham.

This so demoralised Australia that they went a further game down when they lost by 29 runs in the next Test, with Ian Botham taking 5 wickets for only 11 runs in Australia's second innings. Man of the match – Ian Botham.

So here we are at Old Trafford for the fifth Test in a 6 game series. It's Saturday morning and all is quiet. That must mean that Geoffrey Boycott and Chris Tavaré must be at the crease! Just before lunch Boycott was dismissed and Botham came in, swinging the bat in an arc, looking like he was in the mood! He certainly was, and before the day was out he'd scored 118 runs, the hundred coming in just 86 balls, much to the delight of a sell out crowd, me being one of them! To add insult to injury, he smashed Dennis Lillee, one of the greatest fast bowlers of all time, for three of his six, sixes! Man of the match – Ian Botham!

The series ended in a 3-1 win to England over Australia and the Man of the Series? You've guessed – Ian Botham!

Botham was once banned for two months after admitting to smoking cannabis. He was sponsored by Nike at the time and on his return they created an advert which was removed after the British public saw the lighter side. It showed the bottom part of the lower leg with the cricket boot on the playing surface, with the brilliant caption, "Ian Botham – back on the grass!"

One of the lighter sides of cricket over the years has been the commentators, especially of the radio persuasion. The greatest of all being Brian Johnston who probably made more blunders than most.............

"There's Neil Harvey standing at leg slip with his legs wide open, waiting for a tickle!"

"The bowler's Holding the batsman's Willey!"

And the time when he convulsed with laughter for over a minute when Jonathan Agnew suggested that Ian Botham was out 'hit wicket' because he failed to 'get his leg over!'

Prime Time

We were into the third series of Sit Thi Deawn and the BBC decided to put the programme on at Prime Time. The show would run from seven in the evening to seven thirty. This was brilliant because it would give us more exposure to more people. Things got even better when Granada decided that they would go on strike for some unknown reason! The strike coincided almost exactly with our show so the whole of the North-West had only two choices on a Tuesday night; they could watch BBC1 or BBC2. Now, in those days BBC2 was quite highbrow so the viewing public mainly tuned in to our show which broke all audience records for a regional television show.

Everywhere we went we were pointed at, spoken to, verbally abused and generally lauded by all and sundry! It was an amazing time and we certainly knew what 'celebrity' meant. We'd be asked to all sorts of things; opening of stores, nightclubs, garden parties, etc. I was asked to open a new butcher's shop in Ulverston. The journey takes a couple of hours each way and, in gratitude, they gave me two pounds of sausage!

On another occasion, I was asked to open a parish fete in Preston and turned up on time to follow a group of people into a church hall. Several people recognised me and asked, "What on earth are you doing here?"

"I've come to open the garden party", came my reply.

"Well I think you've come to the wrong place!"

"What do you mean?"

"Well I've seen you on telly and I know you like a pint!"

"So?"

"Well, today is the centenary of the National Temperance Federation and we are here to celebrate the signing of the pledge!"

I quickly made my excuses and left!

In 1832, Joseph Livesey and seven other Prestonians signed a pledge that they would never drink alcohol and in 1835 the Temperance Society was founded. Originally, they would only refrain from drinking spirits and would continue to drink wine and beer. In the 1940s however, members would advocate total teetotalism. Besides the Methodists, members of the Catholic Church, Quakers and Salvationists joined in the crusade. The National Temperance Federation was formed in 1884 and became closely linked with the Liberal Party, whereas the Tories tended to support the drinks trade.

George Sims in 1889 said;

"Drink is the curse of these communities: but how is it to be wondered at? The gin-palaces flourish in the slums and fortunes are made of men and women who seldom know where tomorrow's meal is coming from."

So the three little pigs go out for a meal. The first little pig asks the waiter for soup as a starter. The second little piggy chooses prawn cocktail. When asked what he would like for starters, the third little piggy says, "I'd like lots of beer!"

When it comes to the main course, the first little piggy chooses steak, the second little piggy says he would like scampi, whilst the third little piggy says, "Give me lots more beer!"

For sweet the first piggy chooses black forest gateaux, the second piggy has cheese and biscuits, whilst the third little piggy says, "I'd like lots of beer!" The waiter cannot hold back his curiosity any longer and asks the three little piggies, " I hope you've enjoyed your meal little piggies but could I ask a question?"

"Of course!"

"Why did the third little piggy choose beer for every course?"

He replies, "Well I'm the one who shouts wee, wee, wee, all the way home!"

Cruising

We'd worked, by this time, in every conceivable venue, from back rooms in pubs to the largest venues in the North West, so what else was there for us to do?

"Fancy a cruise boys?"

"Where to?"

"Mediterranean and Canary Islands."

"Sounds good; when?"

"Next January, after the panto season!"

So there we were, preparing for a cruise! It all sounded very easy, although payment was non-existent. The cruise itself would be payment if we agreed to do it. We'd need dinner suits and all the paraphernalia for that type of job. We were to sail from Southampton and would be away for 15 days. We would do three shows of one hour over the two weeks and the rest of the time would be ours to do as we wished. So, after a meeting that lasted about ten seconds, we went into Manchester and purchased matching dinner suits.

None of us had ever been on a cruise before so we were quite excited about the prospect of sailing the high seas again. Or should I say that I was quite excited about sailing the high seas again. The other lads were quite nervous following our exploits on the Isle of Man Steam Packet company, previously!

"It's a completely different sort of boat! It will be totally stable and you won't even know it's moving!"

"Is that what they said on the Titanic?"

"Don't be silly, we're not going round the Arctic Circle, we're sailing round the Med!"

"Yeah, but to get to the Med you have to go across the Bay of Biscay!"

Parts of the Continental shelf extend from the west coast of France well into the bay, making the water fairly shallow. This results in rough seas for which the bay is famous. It is home to some of the Atlantic Ocean's fiercest weather caused by powerful windstorms that develop when the pressure falls rapidly. They resemble hurricanes and crash into the bay with maximum power.

I don't think I'd better tell them that though!

So, several months later we drive down to Southampton to join the crew of the ship (I can't remember what it was called) and sail towards the Bay of Biscay! So that you can relate, I'll give it a name! We got to Southampton and walked up the gangplank of the 'Marie Celeste', or was it the 'Black Pearl' with Captain Jack Sparrow at the helm. No we'll stick with 'Marie Celeste'.

The original Marie Celeste was an American/British brigantine which was found abandoned in the Atlantic Ocean in 1872. One lifeboat was missing together with all of the crew, totalling 10, which included the captain's wife and child, aged two. Everything on board was untouched, including enough food for six months, the complete cargo and all valuables. Nobody on board was ever seen again!

She was always classed as a 'cursed' ship following the deaths of three of her captains. Originally named the 'Amazon', her name was changed after being salvaged and repaired in 1869. She set sail from New York to Genoa, Italy on the 7th November 1872 and the last entry in the captain's log was on the 24th day of that month. It was found abandoned on the 4th December 1872 by the Dei Gratia.

So we sleep aboard our Marie Celeste on the night before our departure. We are greeted by the Captain and Head of entertainment the following morning.

"We'll show you around the theatre and introduce you to the other musicians, but apart from that you don't need to do anything for four days!"

From then on in, I was to learn how a cruise worked! You get up in the morning and have breakfast. Once eaten you go back to your cabin and prepare for morning coffee. Almost immediately it's lunch time, followed by afternoon tea! You just have time after that to get suited and booted and ready for dinner. If you've not eaten enough by then don't worry, you can look forward to supper!

In the few minutes you have between meals, the ship provides entertainment competitions and other things to do. I decided to enter the table tennis competition which was an eye opener! Norman and I played quite a bit of table tennis and had both previously played in the local table tennis leagues. In the first round I met an elderly gentleman who was having trouble standing up so it was almost a walkover. Unfortunately, the competition didn't get any better and before I knew it I'd got to the final! Sensibly, Norman had let somebody beat him so he wouldn't have to be as embarrassed as I was going to be!

So, to a great drum roll and fanfare, the finalists of the Marie Celeste table tennis competition were introduced. I strode forward to be greeted by a very elderly lady who was riddled with rheumatoid arthritis! She could hardly hold her bat and I was frightened of shaking hands for fear I would injure my opponent.

Well you can't win this! Whatever you do Tony, you must lose this match but try not to make it too obvious!

The game begins and I realise that just knocking the ball back for her to hit is not going to lose this one! I'm going to have to take more drastic action. So I begin to hit the ball into the net and should I occasionally send it over the net I make it miss the edge of the table. With great difficulty, I manage to lose the match!

As the trophies were presented the old lady leaned towards me and whispered, "You were very kind!"

"No, you won fair and square!" I countered.

She gazed over the trophy and a tear came to her eye. "This is the first thing I've ever won in my life!"

The following day we stop at Lisbon and have a couple of hours to walk from the port and view a couple of Portuguese artefacts before it's time to re-board our vessel. This evening is the night of our first show and we were quite nervous. We'd been travelling full steam ahead all day and been followed by dolphins for several miles. They danced for us and gave a fabulous display!

The word dolphin comes from the Greek, delphis, related to delphus (Greek for womb), hence the fish with a womb! There are forty species from the smallest, Maui's dolphin, to the largest, the Orca or killer whale. They are mainly found in shallower seas where there is a continental shelf, hence their abundance in the Bay of Biscay! That, as a matter of interest, was a damp squib; we had the most pleasant trip across that expanse of sea and the water was like a mirror!

We did our first show later that evening and got a tremendous ovation. Once finished, we were called into the captain's office to be told that Norman's father had died earlier that day. He would, of course, be dropped off at the next port so that he could make his way home.

As the show at the time needed all four of us, it was decided, with the full support of the captain and head of entertainment, that we would all return to England. We left the ship the following day at Seville and got a flight from there to Madrid, followed by an onward flight to Manchester. A sad end to very short adventure!

Doddy's Christmas Extravaganza

We had a phone call from Terry Wheeler, "Alright boys, how's it going?"

"Fine, Terry!"

"Got an idea for a Christmas show!"

"That's great!"

"Sit Thi Deawn?"

"No, I thought we'd do something a bit different!"

"Like?"

"Like a show with Doddy! He'll be lord of the manor and you'll be his minstrels! We'll have some jugglers and a strong man and it will be done in Chester."

"Whereabouts in Chester?"

"At the Guild Hall. It's a marvellous building and it can be Ken Dodd's castle."

"So, does that mean we'll have to dress up?"

"Definitely, we've got some fabulous doublet and hose and wonderful tricornered hats with ostrich feathers!"

"Sounds great, I don't think!"

"It will be marvellous. You'll enjoy every minute! Have you ever worked with Doddy?"

"A couple of times but he tends to go on a bit don't you think?"

"Oh, that's part of his act but he can't do it on telly!"

"Are you sure?"

"Positive!"

"OK, we'll see you there then!"

Ken Dodd is a legend of the British stage. One of the funniest comedians that Britain has ever produced he's been working for six decades to sell-out houses throughout the land.

Born in Knotty Ash, the son of a coal merchant, he was dared by his school friends, at age seven, to ride his bike with his eyes closed. He did it but had an accident that caused facial scars and his distinctive buck teeth. Besides being a comedian, Ken has had nineteen top 40 singles throughout his career, 'Tears' in 1965 becoming the best selling single of that year and number 19 in the top twenty best selling singles of all time in the United Kingdom.

He has also courted controversy during his career. He was tried for tax evasion in 1989. During the trial, it came to light that there was very little money in his bank account but over £300,000 in suitcases scattered around his bedroom. When asked by the judge;

"What does a hundred thousand pounds in a suitcase feel like?"

Doddy replied, "The notes are very light M'lord!"

He was defended by the leading English barrister of the day, George Carmen who famously said, "Some accountants are comedians, but comedians are never accountants!"

He was acquitted of all charges!

I'm sure when the judge released him he was tattifelariously discumknockerated and waved his tickling stick around the court saying , "How tickled I am!"

Several years later, he was to appear in court for a completely different reason when a woman, Ruth Tagg, was accused of stalking him. She pleaded guilty to harassment and arson, after sending threatening letters, a dead rat and burning rags through his letter box.

Doddy continues to work to the present day and his shows are legendary. We appeared as his guest on one recently. The show started at seven o'clock and finished at quarter to one in the morning! The man should have more sense at his age!

So the show went ahead at Christmas. We were all dressed in medieval costumes for the Lord of the manor who was played by Ken. We'd sing a few songs for him during dinner which consisted of dozens of plastic geese, ducks and turkeys. The room was decorated with Christmas trees and ornaments, even though they didn't come into use in England until the reign of Queen Victoria! There were jugglers, acrobats, clowns and strong men who made it a right festive occasion.

So, it's Christmas Eve and Santa is having a disastrous day. His little helpers had gone on strike for more pay and better working conditions. The reindeer had been in the pub all day and had far too much to drink, hence Rudolph's nose! Everyone was complaining about everything when Santa starts to lose his patience, "Now come on you lot, I treat you all very well and I'm having nothing but trouble. I've got to deliver millions of presents this evening so I want you lot to buck up!"

There's a grumble of discontent amongst his staff as Santa continues, "And I've sent that fairy out for a Christmas tree but I've not seen hide nor hair of her for hours. What's this place coming to?"

Just then the door creaks open and a dishevelled looking fairy covered in snow walks into the room, dragging a Christmas tree behind her. She screams, "Hey fatty! Where do you want this tree sticking?"

And so began the tradition of the Christmas fairy's place on top of the tree!

Front Page News

The only time I'd managed to get on the front page of a newspaper occurred around this time. Denis had decided that he'd had enough of travelling around the UK and so called time on the Weavers. He was replaced by a fresh faced young bloke from just down the road in Culcheth, near Warrington. Jeff Hill was a singer songwriter and the most pleasant bloke you could ever wish to meet! He was always quiet and unassuming, unless someone rubbed him up the wrong way!

As a duo, we occasionally did some gigs, usually for charity. We had recorded several albums under the pseudonym of 'Blueberry Hill' and had been asked to appear at various venues but mostly refused as our allegiances were totally with the group. However, a woman approached us one evening and asked if we could appear at a charity function for a children's ward in the local hospital.

"Are you asking for the two of us or the whole group?"

"Oh, just the two of you. It's at a Labour Club in Bolton and you'll be top of the bill! We'll have a few comedians on and a couple of singers so it should be a good night. They are all coming for nothing – how much do you want?"

I'm sure that this is the only business that people expect you to work for nothing on a regular basis! You wouldn't ask your local plumber or electrician if they would come round to your house and work for nothing. Maybe you would do it for a close friend but not for someone you meet on a night out!

"Sure, we'll come for nothing!"

"Great, see you on the night."

So, several weeks later we turn up to the venue to see Houghton Weavers posters all over the place! They are

accompanied by signs that read, 'appearing here tonight!"
Both Jeff and I are a bit apprehensive and ask the lady in
charge if they have been advertising the whole group.

"It doesn't matter, it's for charity!"

"But that isn't the point", came my reply, "you've
advertised the whole group when you know full well that there
would be only two of us!"

"So what? Just get on that stage and do your bit!"

"Excuse me please", came my reply, "I think it is only fair
that you get up on the stage and tell everybody that the whole
group were never invited this evening. People will think that
only half of us have turned up because it doesn't matter."

The organiser now becomes a bit ratty, "Get on that
'effing' stage now or I'll have your name all over the Evening
News tomorrow!"

"Whoah, whoah, this is getting ridiculous! We've agreed to
come here tonight, free of charge and all we are asking is that
the audience know who were invited. We don't want to give
our group a bad name."

"I'll give you all a bad name if you don't get out there. I
know the editor of the Bolton Evening News and I'm warning
you to get on that 'effing' stage or else I'll have your pictures
plastered all over the news!"

"Excuse me please! I think the newspapers would like to
hear our side of the story and when they realise that we are
being abused they might have something to say on our
behalf!"

How wrong was I!

"Don't be so bloody soft and get out there or else!"

"I'm not standing for this!" retorts Jeff, "We are doing you
the favour, not the other way around and I'm not being spoken
to like that, so I'm off!"

He leaves through the changing room door.

"See what you've done you stupid woman!"

"This is your last chance; get on that stage or I'll tell every
'effing' newspaper I know that you've refused to do a charity
for poor unfortunate kids!"

"I'm sorry", came my reply, "but I've got to stick by my
friend, not a loud mouthed drunk who I don't know!" and I
followed Jeff onto the car park.

The following night she was right and my face was on the front page of the Bolton Evening News with the caption, "Houghton Weaver refuses to do a charity night for dying children!" It went on to say that I had adamantly refused to go on stage even though the organisers had pleaded with me to do so. Many in the audience said they would never go to watch the group again!

I immediately rang the newspaper and told them about the previous evening but they weren't bothered. They had their scoop and they were sticking by it. I explained that it hadn't happened as they had reported it and demanded that they made a correction; which they duly did; on page 27 on the bottom of the column! I sympathise with many 'A' standard celebrities who have lies printed about them every day. This was the only time I've had a run in with the papers. Since that time I have done innumerable charity nights but none of them have managed to get on the front page yet!

Chicken Coop

Whilst we are talking about charity nights; I remember one in Blackpool where we appeared with the Nolan Sisters and Frank Carson. Both these acts have their origin in Ireland. Originally from Dublin, Tommy and Maureen Nolan, who were both professional singers, brought their family over to Blackpool and formed 'The Nolan family'. Mother and dad eventually retired and the Nolan sisters were formed. They had a tremendous amount of success and had a massive hit with 'I'm in the Mood for Dancing' in 1979 which reached number three in the UK charts. Probably one of the highlights of their career was when they supported Frank Sinatra on a European tour.

Frank Carson, on the other hand was from Belfast and became a very popular act in the Province before moving to Blackpool, where he won Opportunity Knocks three times before starring in Johnny Hamp's 'Comedians'. He appeared many times on 'The Wheeltappers and Shunters Social Club' and was a regular guest on Saturday morning's TISWAS. His most famous lines were, 'It's the way I tell 'em!" and 'It's a Cracker!" although my favourite was, "two boiled eggs!"

We had all agreed to appear at a farm on the Fylde, near Poulton, for a local charity. Little did we know that we were appearing in a chicken coop! It was a huge wooden shed that had been converted, for the evening, into a cabaret lounge. There had been chickens in it a few hours previously and every time anybody moved there was a flurry of feathers! The place reeked of chicken droppings and the only way we got through the night was because everyone who was appearing had a tremendous sense of fun. Frank was constantly telling gags and the Nolans were just as quick! "I don't think my wife likes me!" quipped Frank, "I had a heart attack the other day and she wrote for an ambulance!"

"Men are like bank accounts," announces Bernie, "without a lot of money, they don't generate much interest!" We had a great night despite the things that were sent to try us!

"Just as a matter of interest, does anybody know where we can get changed?"

"No idea! More importantly, where are we performing?"

Just then, the organiser, accompanied by the farmer, walk into the room.

"Thank you all so much for coming here tonight! Can I show you the stage?"

"Stage? You've got a stage?"

"Oh yes, my wife and I built it this afternoon, after we'd cleared out the chickens."

"By the way, where are they?"

"In the coop next door until tomorrow!" came his reply. We walk through the shed and find a large piece of plywood, on top of a dozen or so beer crates! Hanging in front of this health and safety catastrophe is a large sheet of tarpaulin.

"We've even got you a curtain!" came the animated reply from our friendly Old MacDonald! "And lights!"

Nailed to the wall on the side of the shed are two large halogen lamps that are probably used on the farm during the night! Within two minutes of being on stage we will probably all be electrocuted or fried to death!

"Well done!" cries Frank, "No expense spent I see!"

"We've tried to make an effort," replies the farmer jovially.

"Not to worry! We'll make the best it! How much are tickets?"

"Fifty pounds each", comes the reply.

"Fifty bloody pounds, for a night with chicken droppings and feathers!"

"Yes, it's sold out!"

"My God, we'd better give them a good night."

"I'm sure you will. Would you like to see your changing room?"

"I'm afraid to say yes!" comes a whisper from a Nolan sister.

"I've rigged up a dressing room in one of the cowsheds!"

"No chance! That's going a bit too far!"

"Only joking, you can change in the house."

"Thank goodness for that!"

So the changing facilities were fine, the audience were great and joined in the fun, even though most of them were in evening wear!

As the night progressed, it got hotter and hotter. The chicken droppings began to cook and the whole room took on a wonderful ambience that is difficult to relay to you in words! Most of the people left with more than they came in with and many years later, people who attended the evening, could still remember one thing about the night.....the smell! Not Frank Carson, not the Nolans, not the Weavers but the smell of the chicken coop in Blackpool!

South Pier

Another night in Blackpool springs to mind when I begin to reminisce. We had been booked to appear at the South Pier in the resort, as Top of the Bill, in a summer spectacular. We were to do the whole of the second half whilst the first half would have a compere/comedian, a solo singer and a magician.

The show began with the orchestra (well organist, drummer and bass!) in the pit playing background music whilst the audience take to their seats. The curtains open and the compere welcomes everyone to the theatre. He tells gags for about fifteen minutes and introduces the first act, the magician! As we are only performing in the second half, we've sneaked into the back row to watch the show.

To a magnificent drum roll and fanfare our magician appears on stage. But this is no ordinary magician, who makes doves and budgerigars appear! No, this magician pulls chickens, geese and owls from every conceivable hidey hole! There's a turkey, a duck, a parrot and one or two species that I couldn't recognise. The act is utter chaos and the whole audience are in raptures with the confusion of it all. Birds are appearing everywhere and the finale is reached when he brings a huge bird of prey out of his jacket!

The audience are going berserk as the curtain closes to an ecstatic round of applause. On walks the compere and tells a couple of stories before introducing the solo singer who will be entertaining the crowd in front of the curtain. A stage hand walks on and places a tall stool behind the microphone as another helper brings on a guitar and stand. The soloist walks to the centre of the stage, to a ripple of applause and begins to introduce the first song, "A lovely ballad recorded by Barry Manilow."

He gets about three lines into the song and everyone hears a loud, 'cock a doodle doo!' followed by the curtain behind him billowing out and a voice shouting, "Come here you bugger!"

Confusion reigns behind the back-drop as the poor singer tries in vain to get the audience on his side. All they are interested in is the chaos going on behind him as the magician tries in vain to contain all his charges! You can hear footsteps and a clattering of scenery followed by bird calls of every kind! The climax is reached when we hear an almighty yelp from behind the curtain, followed by the scream of a feathered beast, a couple of bangs on the tabs, followed by silence for a couple of seconds. Then in slow motion, a white feather, falling, very slowly, to the right then to the left and finishing on the nose of the unfortunate singer, doing an impression of Barry Manilow. Some bright spark in the crowd shouted, "Good job he's doing Manilow ....got the nose for it!"

Radio 2

We were offered a series on Radio Two: the first series was recorded at the Hulme 'Playhouse', a building with a chequered past. It was originally called the Hippodrome, then the Grand Junction and became the Playhouse before the BBC bought the building in 1956. They used it as a radio and television studio until 1987, from whence it became the NIA centre and today is being refurbished as a church. There was a small cafe upstairs where they made snacks and drinks for the performers. I once remember Alan Fawkes diving into a cucumber sandwich during a break from recording. When we resumed, Alan had terrible wind and belched his way through the rest of the show, much to the amusement of Richie Close and his band!

After several shows all the recordings moved to the fabulous Coliseum Theatre, in Oldham. This marvellous theatre was built in 1885 as a Grand American Circus theatre and was surrounded by a dozen other auditoriums, all of which have now disappeared. Some of its past performers include Charlie Chaplin, Stan Laurel, Dame Thora Hird and Eric Sykes. It was closed in 1931 due to the world wide recessions but reopened in 1939 and became home of the Oldham Repertory Company. Many young actors, who now feature in the likes of 'Coronation Street' and 'Emmerdale' began their careers in this lovely little place.

Our show was recorded in front of a live audience and featured mainstream comics such as Jim Bowen, Mick Miller and Mike Harding to name a few. The BBC van parked alongside the loading bay and the crew brought hundreds of electrical cables through the back door, onto the stage. We would record a couple of shows each night so that the audience could be entertained for a couple of hours; longer if we got it wrong! There was a television screen in the van so that the producer could see what was going on. Over the six series we did, there were two producers, Dave Shannon and John Leonard, both talented folk performers in their own right. We had Richie Close and his backing band to augment our music, or to play for the comedians who like to sing a song, or use a musical accompaniment to their act.

One of these momentous recordings just happened to coincide with a personal milestone – my fortieth birthday. As a prank, the rest of the lads had arranged, without my knowledge, to employ the services of a 'strip-o-gram', which they thought would be extremely embarrassing for me and enjoyable for the audience. The producer and everybody else of importance were aware of what was about to happen with strict instructions that the 'strip-o-gram' would absolutely not 'strip'!

So, halfway through the show, to the amusement of my fellow performers and much bemusement of a packed audience, this poor girl walks onto stage and peers out front!

"Bloody hell! It's full!" she screams in my ear.

"Don't worry love," I try to calm her, "I'll do whatever you want, as long as it's legal! Don't look at them, just keep your eyes on me!"

So this poor girl tries to go through the routine that she usually performs to about twenty blokes in the back room of a pub! Unfortunately, for her, there are almost six hundred men, women and children trying to work out how this escapade will unfold. Fortunately, she gets into the swing of things (I don't mean that literally) and begins to enjoy herself. This is by far the biggest audience of her career! She prances around the stage and tries to make me nervous but the only nervous ones were the rest of the group and herself. Eventually her dance finishes and she leaves to rapturous applause and several encores.

After the debacle, she actually asked if she could appear regularly on our stage shows but sadly, we declined. The BBC, on the other hand, offered us several more series which we agreed to overwhelmingly!

195

Guests

Over the years, we have had many guests joining us on stage, usually during our Christmas shows which we began to embark on following six pantomimes. Several winners of television talent shows, including the all time winner of 'Opportunity Knocks', Berni Flint, Rosser and Davies from the 'Valleys' in Wales and Paul McCoy who won the final of 'Stars in their Eyes' as Gilbert O'Sullivan have joined us over the years, together with lots of other friends.

One of our all time favourites is our very own 'Bolton Bullfrog' , Bernard Wrigley. Bernard was joined on stage by another 'Lancashire Lad', Dave Dutton, actor, writer and general nutcase. They had jointly written an alternative 'nativity' play, in the words of the children they would be playing. Bernard played the part of Mary, with his deep 'Lanky' twang and beard! Joseph was to be Dave's part and he played it with relish. When talking about the child to be born, Joseph asks Mary what the child's name should be. Mary answers, "I think I fancy Dwayne!"

Joseph reaches into his smock and pulls out a bottle of beer. "What on earth is that Joseph?, asks Mary. To which Joseph replies, "Ale! Mary". Absolutely no disrespect intended in any way. The Bishop of Salford found it highly amusing! Bernard, to me, is an incredibly talented individual, who, like Billy Connolly, Jasper Carrot and Mike Harding, who all come from the same folk background, takes an alternative look at the funny side of life. And they have all been doing it long before 'alternative' comedy came to the fore.

Dave Dutton, on the other hand is a highly amusing monologue writer. I remember once sitting in a dentist's waiting room, reading a five year old copy of Lancashire Life, when I came across one of his poems that had recently won the Fylde Folk Festival's top award for poetry. The monologue is about a gentleman named Thrumble, who plays trombone. One line, near the end of the piece goes something like this.....

'His old trombone's seen better days, it's like us all by gum. It's old and bent and has more dents, than a one eyed joiner's thumb!'

Magic!

Whilst I'm on the Christmas theme, we regularly relate the time that Hughie Jones from the 'Spinners' joined us on Christmas Eve one year. The Spinners were an incredibly successful group who formed in 1957 as the 'Gin Mill Skiffle Group' and became the Spinners in September of the following year. Not many people know that a great friend of ours, Jacqueline MacDonald was an original member of the group. They produced over 40 albums and recorded for both Philips Records and EMI. Although they retired in 1988, they re-formed in 1989 to lead the community singing at the FA cup Final between Liverpool and Everton. A little piece of sporting history was made when Stuart McCall became the first substitute to score two goals in an FA Cup Final. However, two minutes later, Ian Rush equalled his feat to score the winning goal. Liverpool won three two in extra-time.

Going back to my friend Hughie Jones! He was the only member of the Spinners to be born in Liverpool and came onto stage to introduce his song. Outside, there was a thunderstorm taking place. The roof of the stage was of metal construction and as the hailstones battered noisily overhead, together with the flashes of lightning and cracks of thunder, Hughie bravely warbled his way through 'Silent Night'!

My favourite guest of all time though, is my brother! James, Jim or Jimmy, depending on your relationship with him, was always the one in my family who would make it into show business. He bought a guitar as a child and began to write songs. He's always sung and entertained wherever he went and it was assumed that he would be the one to be a professional entertainer. I, on the other hand, fell into it. I've always loved singing and I got lucky. My brother can still be seen today in the villages of the Dordogne in France, where, when he feels the urge, he'll go onto the streets and 'busk' the days away.

Changes

During the many years we've been together we have had a couple of changes. I've mentioned Jeff Hill, who joined us after eight years but our most recent acquisition is Steve Millington, a musical genius from Acton Bridge in Cheshire. Steve has played all over the world with many illustrious acts but eventually came down to earth and joined us! For many years before joining the Weavers, Steve played with an extremely successful country music band named 'Poacher'. The group won the final of another talent show called 'New Faces' and went on to become the top British country music act for 5 consecutive years between 1978 and 1983. They have toured with Country legends Don Williams and Tammy Wynette and were the original backing band for current country great, Sarah Jorey.

The tale I tell relates to Steve working with Poacher at the Wembley Country Music Festival, probably the biggest of its kind in this country. The show was filmed for a world-wide audience and was 'live' on BBC2 and Sky television.

"As the show was to be televised live, we did several rehearsals of the finale, all of which went well. We made an appearance from behind the central curtain, walked to the front of the stage where we took a bow, then walked backwards to our final spot on the side of the stage, as the next act appeared centrally and did the same. We'd gone down well in the actual show, so when we took the final bow, there was rapturous applause from the ten thousand people in the auditorium. I bowed with the rest of the group and took one step backwards and fell flat on my backside in front of 10,000 people and on live television!"

It's always the mistakes you remember!

Norman left the group in 1999 to pursue a solo career and Jeff left several years later leaving myself, David and Steve to continue. Because there have been these few changes, people get quite confused and ask things like, "When did the black bloke leave?"

I'd reply, "We've never had a black bloke in our group, that's the Spinners; Cliff the West Indian guy from Cuba!"

"No, Houghton Weavers, I've been watching you lot since 1967!"

"No you haven't!"

"Yes, I have!"

"No you haven't. We didn't start until 1975!"

"Are you sure?"

"Of course I'm sure, I'm the singer!"

"Well then, when did that woman leave?"

"What woman?"

"The one who used to sing with you."

"We've never had a woman!"

"Yes, you have! Are you sure you've been singing with the group a long time?"

"Of course I am. I started the bloody group!"

"Well, when did that woman leave?"

"We've never had a woman, I think you mean Linda Meeks from the 'Fivepenny Piece'"

"No, you used to have a woman! When did she leave?"

"The same time as the black guy!" comes my reply.

Over the Years

Since the group began I've been married twice and have three wonderful children of whom I think the world of; daughter Amy, the oldest and sons Tom and Jack. My personal life is exactly what it says but there are one or two tales I can relate about growing up. When my daughter was about eighteen months old, the family went on holiday to Lake Como in the Italian lakes. Our hotel was perched on a hillside, so the gardens and swimming pool at the rear of the establishment were rather unsuitable for children, as it was quite rocky and filled with a fragrant garden. One afternoon as we walked by the pool, I was holding hands with Amy as we tried to make our way through the rocks and plants. Quite suddenly, she forced her hand from mine and jumped!

She landed in the deep end of the pool and quite rapidly sank to the bottom! In less than a second, I followed her, fully clothed, in utter panic, into the depths. For what seemed an eternity I paddled, until I eventually reached her, grabbed her by the waist and rapidly swam to the surface!

We burst to the surface together. I was fully ready to perform mouth to mouth on my baby and rush her to hospital, when she gasped, blew out a mouthful of water, opened her eyes wide and shouted, "Again!"

Several years later, I had remarried and my wife, Andrea, was heavily pregnant with her second child. We had arranged to go away for the weekend to an outward bound centre in North Wales with a group of friends. Andrea would go, with Tom, our eldest, on Friday night and I would join them the following morning, as I had a gig with the group. I left bright and early on Saturday morning and drove to meet a friend in the town of Conway, as I was unsure of the road layout up the mountainous retreat. I arrived around 7.30 am. to be greeted by my friend. "Tony, I've got some bad news! We are not going up to the centre but to the hospital. It appears that everybody's been poisoned!"

"What do you mean?"

"Well you know Keith and Steve?"

"Of course!"

"Well they both worked down the pit and noticed the signs!"

"What bloody signs?"

"Well they think we've all got carbon monoxide poisoning. There were about fifteen sleeping in the west wing and they all woke up feeling sick!"

"Is everybody else alright?"

"Seems so but we'll go straight to the hospital at Llandudno."

"Lead the way!"

Carbon monoxide is a colourless, odourless and tasteless but highly toxic gas. The signs of poisoning are headache, dizziness and nausea. It can lead to toxicity of the nervous system and the heart and can have very severe effects on the foetus of a pregnant woman.

We arrive at the cottage hospital to find that the whole of the Welsh National Health Service has been put on red alert. All our friends are together in a small ward and there are doctors and nurses from all over Wales. We were told that there was a chance that nobody would be adversely affected because of the rapid response of the miners in our midst. However, they would all have to go through the decompression chamber at Ellesmere Port on the Wirral. The doctors said that the carbon monoxide would stay in the blood stream unless it was forced out. This would need a five hour stay in the decompression chamber. Another one of the women on the holiday was equally as pregnant as my wife and was being air lifted by helicopter to get to the decompression chamber as quickly as possible.

It emerged that my wife had woken during the night and had come downstairs for a drink of water and stayed. She had accidentally saved herself from more serious harm. It was thought that the lighting was to blame. All the heating and lighting in the building was powered by 'propane' gas bottles and it was later proved to be the culprit. Everyone involved had to go through decompression but I'm happy to say that all made a full recovery, including both pregnant women and their unborn children. I'm not sure if the incident had some effect on my unborn son, Jack, but he is a very strange young man! Only kidding!

They've grown up as most kids, having their ups and downs! The memorable events have been the problems! Falling off a bike and breaking a few fingers, followed by the head being glued together! Walking into the sea with a brand new iphone in their pocket! Winning and losing at football, swimming and cricket. Winning and losing with their musical exploits. Worrying over exam results – the usual things!

Many memorable nights have passed by during our four decades. We've worked in some amazing venues, each one of them with their own personality. Some slightly less grand than others! We've travelled around Britain and less so in Europe and we've met some amazing people. We've worked with fabulous acts and not so fabulous acts. We've met some very famous and not so famous people who have all added to the tapestry of our career. As the years have gone by and our audiences have shrunk, we continue to do what it says on the tin, 'Keep Folk Smiling'. On the whole, most of our audiences have liked what we've done and we hope to continue doing for many more years to come. To them all, I'd like to extend my thanks and gratitude for making me a very lucky man, doing a job that, on the whole, has been an absolute pleasure. Little did we know, when we were practicing for the very first time, in the kitchen of David's house, that we'd still be attempting to get it right almost forty years later!

Cheers!